THE GALLOWAYS:

PIONEERS, PLANTERS AND PATRIOTS

Patton Gardenier Galloway

Raleigh, North Carolina

3rd Edition 2015

isbn 978-1-300-03466-7

Published by lulu.com

CONTENTS

Preface

This is a selective story about one line of my ancestry. It is not a genealogy, for it doesn't try to include all of these ancestors. Nor is it a history, for it describes only selected events, as they affect selected people. Nor is it strictly confined to ancestors, as considerable space is given to some Galloways who, while related, are not our direct progenitors.

The bits and pieces that fit together to make up this story have been collected over many years and from many sources including journals and diaries by a few ancestors who were farsighted enough to leave such records; memories and family tales; court and church records; census and tax lists; and historical and genealogical publications. There are numerous footnotes which identify sources for anyone who wants to dig deeper into a particular chapter.

Except as noted, only reasonably reliable sources have been used, but even primary sources aren't always accurate; early records are sometimes careless about spelling and dates. And, while reliable sources make up the bones of this story, imagination and speculation are sometimes used to fill in gaps and make sense out of scattered clues. Care has been taken to state when this happens.

Every effort has been made to show our ancestors as they really were- which is not always a pretty story. These are fascinating and diverse people who, collectively, contributed to the growth of our Nation by exploring and settling her wilderness, serving in her wars, and farming her land. They were men and women of strong opinions and the will to stand behind them, people of integrity and commitment. They were restless people, moving from place to place in pursuit of religious freedom, new opportunities, and new adventures.

This is not a finished document, nor can it ever be. Anyone pursuing this kind of research will continue to come up with a new clue, a new name, a new date, or a new fact that should be included, or that sheds new light on the tangled webs of the past.

I wish to express my deep gratitude to my cousin Thomas Roddy Galloway for his invaluable contributions to the content of this project, as well as his unflagging encouragement over many years, and to my son, Charles Samuel Galloway and to John Peters for their technical support in preparing this for publication.

Patton Gardenier Galloway
Raleigh, North Carolina

Chapter 1

British Homelands

Every family shares traits that are passed down from generation to generation. While these may fade as they are diluted by time and by marriage, most of us take pride in those characteristics that we view as part of our heritage. This narrative will trace one branch of the Galloways back from Kentucky and Pennsylvania to Maryland and then Virginia, then further back to the British Isles. But first, a quick look at the land and the history that forged this family's characteristic traits.

The Scottish Lowlands

Galloway was first a placename: "land of the foreign gaels." This area comprises the southwestern corner of Scotland, cut off from England by the wide Solway Firth. However, the people of Galloway originally came not from Scotland, but from Ulster, a group of counties in northern Ireland. It is a short sail across the Irish Sea to Galloway and, from the Stone Age down through the 18th Century, there was an almost constant cross-migration between the two areas.

Galloway is rich in remains of prehistoric settlements. Cairn Holy, a mysterious group of standing stones, dates from about 2,000 B.C.. Ruins remain of hill forts built by Iron Age people. The Celts, retreating northward as the Belgic tribes invaded England, came later and built forts and towns, ruled by warrior kings.

In the First Century A.D., Romans invaded the British Isles.

As their legions pushed north into Scotland, they met such fierce resistance that they were forced to pull back, and Galloway became part of a buffer area between the native Picts to the North and the invading Romans to the South. In the Fifth Century, the Romans were forced to leave Britain and return to Rome, called home to defend their homeland against barbarian hordes pouring in from Asia. Without the Romans to keep order, England was harassed by raiders from Scotland and Ireland. To counter this threat, Saxon tribes from Germany were encouraged to immigrate. These newcomers, called Anglo-Saxons, soon controlled England, but, like the Romans, never managed to exert their control as far north as Galloway.

Although Galloway's location protected it from these successive invasions, it endured frequent raids by people known as Scotti, from across the Irish Sea. By the Fifth Century, these Scotti had colonized the area that is now Galloway. The region evolved as part of the kingdom of Dalriada, which soon extended its military and cultural sway over most of southwestern Scotland. Dalriada, in turn, eventually merged into a Kingdom of Strathclyde, a confederation which was formed to fend off incursions by the Anglo-Saxons who were swarming over England.

A new threat arose in the Ninth Century, when men from Norway began to raid the northern coasts of the British Isles. They returned again and again to plunder, rape and pillage, always without warning and always without mercy, while the native peoples were too weak and disorganized to offer effective resistance. By mid-century, these land-hungry Vikings began to settle in northern Ireland and Scotland, often marrying or mating with local women and producing a new breed, of mixed parentage.

The "Gall-Gaels" who gave their name to Galloway were a product of this Viking incursion: the "Gallgaidhel" or "stranger" (i.e., renegade) Gaels. Some of them were Irishmen who renounced Christianity to join with the heathen invaders; some were of mixed Norse and native parentage; and some were native children who had been reared by Norsemen. This blending of race, culture and religion produced a warlike people, who fought indiscriminately against the Norsemen, the Irish, and anyone else they encountered. By the mid-Ninth Century, they had their own armies and leaders; one recorded battle about that time ended when the Irish King of Ailech defeated the Gallgaidhel fleet and carried off many heads as trophies.

From 1034 until 1066, Galloway was ruled by Jarl (earl) Thorfinn, called the "skull-cleaver," son of the King of Norway. But Norse power in the British Isles came to an abrupt end when the Viking chief Harald Hardrada was decisively defeated by King Harold of England. Harold then marched his men south to meet an invasion by William of Normandy, where he was defeated at the Battle of Hastings. The Norman Conquest of England followed and the Normans, who were themselves descended from Vikings, moved north to the Scottish borders, building a string of forts as they went.

The people of Galloway fought to stay free of both the Normans invading from the south and the Scottish Picts from the north. At the decisive Battle of the Standard in 1311, Galloway men demanded and won the right to lead the assault, many falling under a storm of Norman arrows.

But these fierce fighters were eventually brought under Scottish rule. In 1175, when Fergus, Lord of Galloway, died, King William of Scotland divided Galloway between Fergus' sons, Gilbert and Uchtred. Gratitude was not among these brothers' virtues; when King William was captured by an English army, the brothers and their men deserted his cause and went home to Galloway, where they quickly proceeded to expel the King's officers and to massacre, impartially, all the Irish and Normans they could find. This done, Gilbert, who didn't want to share the throne, had his brother put to death. King William regained the Scottish throne after swearing fealty to King Henry II of England, but Henry used his authority as overlord to free Gilbert, who then drove William's men out of Galloway.

Galloway was soon brought back under Scottish rule, but

continued to be a trouble spot for both English and Scottish overlords. In the 1240's, Henry's successor sent armies there to put down rebellions, as did King Edward in 1300. Galloway was bitterly contested in the wars of independence. Later, men of Galloway fought with Robert the Bruce at Bannockburn, when he wrested the throne of Scotland back from the English.

This brief summary mentions only a few milestones in the bloody history of Galloway, but shows how its history shaped the character of its people. Fighting was their normal occupation. In the rare intervals between wars or rebellions, Galwegians would head south on raids to seize cattle in northern England. Peace and stability were slow to reach the Borders. Even the livestock is distinct, for Galloway gave its name to a breed of beef cattle, sturdy little beasts with coats of curly dark hair, and to a breed of small, tough horses.

Galloway's Sons and Sites

The surname Galloway comes from the placename. In the Eleventh Century, a Scottish king created his country's first earls by ordering his chief subjects to follow the custom of other nations and adopt surnames based on their territorial possessions.[1] One of these "surenames" was Galloway.

Records show persons bearing the name Galloway in Scotland as early as the Thirteenth Century, albeit with varied spellings, as was common in early times. In 1230, Thomas de Galwethia, Earl of Atholl, made a gift of lands to the Abbey of Neubotle. About the same time, Michael de Galewath[ia] was recorded as a witness. In 1405, John Galway was listed as master of a ship belonging to Sir John of Mountgomery. In 1488, Sande Galowey was guilty of 'twllye' (disturbance) in Lanark. In 1597, John Galloway in Kilmaronok was sued for contempt.[2] (Incidentally, the name Patton Galloway is not unique to the present writer. In one of those improbable coincidences with which history is replete, "Pattoun Gallowey" was recorded by the Monastery of Cupar-Angus in 1550 as owning two acres in Carsegrange.)

The Galloway homeland has many claims to distinction. It was the birthplace of Robert the Bruce, who led the long struggle for Scotland's freedom. The first Christian church in Scotland was established there by Saint Ninian. It is rich in literary associations. When Sir Walter Scott's young Lochinvar came out of the West, he rode from Cardoness Castle, near Kircudbright; the grim tower still stands, impregnable except for infrequent sunbeams that invade through the high, slit windows. Scott's Bride of Lammamoor lived at Glen Luce. Dumfries was home to Scotland's revered poet, Robert Burns. Maxwelton's "bonny braes," where Annie Laurie gave her promise true, are in Galloway, as are the sands of Dee, where luckless Mary called the cattle home.

In 1983, when the present writer visited Galloway, few traces were left of its violent past. Instead, a tourist brochure accurately described it as boasting "150 miles of coastline, peaceful seaside villages, lush farmland in the midst of which small villages built from the local granite stand clean and bright among the verdant fields, and [where] a gentle colour-wash seems to lie over everything like a water colour painting brought to life." Sir Walter Scott's description of the land, written a century and a half earlier in his novel *Guy Mannering*, still applied:

The landscape showed a pleasing alteration of hill and dale. . . the vales seemed well cultivated, the little enclosures into which they were divided skirting the bottom of the hills. . . Above these were green pastures, tenanted chiefly by herds of black cattle. . . The remoter hills were of a sterner character, and, at still greater distance, swelled into mountains of dark heath, bordering the horizon with a screen which gave a defined and limited boundary to the cultivated country, and added, at the same time, the pleasing idea, that it was sequestered and solitary. The seacoast corresponded in variety and beauty with the inland view.

Galloway, which encompasses the counties of Wigton and Kircudbright, is called "the Highlands of the Lowlands." The coast is washed by the Gulf Stream, so the climate is much milder than the rest of Scotland. In fact, it looks much like Maryland and central Kentucky: the places where Galloways first settled in America.

Ulster: County Antrim

Galloway was settled mostly by people from Ireland, but, over the centuries, people traveled both directions across the Irish Sea. The people known as "Scotch-Irish" were Lowland Presbyterian Scots who settled in Ulster, a group of counties in northern Ireland. Many came as part of King James I's "Great Plantation" of 1613-15, wherein lowland Scots were settled on lands taken from rebellious Catholics,[3] although some were earlier arrivals and some came later. Among them were some Galloways, most of whom settled in County Antrim.

One incursion, in the early 1600's, was triggered when an Irish chief named Con O'Neill ran short of wine and decided to liberate some casks that had been impounded for non-payment of duties. Fighting ensued and he landed in prison. His desperate wife contacted a nobleman in Ayrshire, just north of Galloway, and offered him half of Con's lands if he would arrange his escape. He did so by hiding a rope in a hollowed-out cheese and smuggling it into the prisoner's cell. With the aid of a friend who had connections at court, the two men then obtained the King's patent, which was needed to ensure their title to the land, in return for which they agreed to "plant" it with Scottish and English colonists.

Scots who settled in Ireland found themselves in a cultural limbo, being neither English nor Irish. The English relied on them to put down rebellions among the solidly-Catholic Irish, who resented the Protestant incursion. But, at the same time, the English persecuted these Scotch-Irish because they were Presbyterians who did not accept the Church of England. The English barred them from office and imposed oppressive rents and tithes, while the Irish regarded them as usurpers.

In this hostile environment, the Scotch-Irish became ready recruits for agents who traveled around Ulster in the mid-18th Century, offering free passage to America for those who would sign up as indentured servants, usually for a term of seven years. At the end of that time, they would be set free and would often be given land of their own, in a country where the hand of English authority lay lightly and where opportunities were unlimited. The resulting exodus was so great that, by the time of the American Revolution, Ulster was all but emptied of its Presbyterian population.[4]

This 18th Century exodus included some Galloways. Not only do American immigration records show some Ulster Galloways, but the 1685 will of a Maryland settler left personalty to a relative in Galloway, Ireland; while the placename no longer exists, this proves that Galloways once lived there. But our line of Galloways apparently was not part of this exodus, nor was they even Ulstermen. They had come to America much earlier and they came not from Ulster, or even from Galloway, but from London.

Galloways in London

The first Galloways to arrive in America were William, in 1623, and Richard and Mary, in 1646. Their arrival in Virginia is well documented, but not their place of origin, although this almost certainly was London. Almost all of the ships that came to Virginia in the early years sailed from there, although they sometimes took on passengers at ports along the way, so almost all of the settlers who arrived before 1650 were Londoners.

The Mormon Church has compiled and sorted English parish records according to surnames. A search of these files turns up a William and Richard Galloway who may well be the Virginia arrivals. However, it should be cautioned that the Mormon lists, while extensive, are neither complete nor necessarily accurate; many parish records have been lost or destroyed over the centuries, and even the diligent Mormons may have overlooked some records.

There had been Galloways in London since at least 1540, when John Galloway married Katheryn Awsten at Saint Margaret's, a church which is located alongside Westminster Abbey, and which holds the grave of Sir Walter Raleigh, whose "lost Colony" was the first English Settlement in the New World. This is the first known church record of a Galloway, except for an Alles (an early spelling of Alice?) who was christened in Lancastershire the same year. Westminster was the site of King Henry VIII's principal palace and of the great Abbey, which dominated not only the landscape, but most aspects of life.

The wedding couple, John and Katheryn, were probably the parents of a William Galloway who was christened at St. Margaret's in 1542 and who grew up to marry Gertrude Betts in 1565 at nearby Saint Martin's in the Fields. This marriage is also recorded under the name of Guiliemus (the Latin version of William) Gallaway, illustrating the wide latitude found in the spelling of names.

In 1565, a John Galloway married Amy Addams at Saint Dunstan's in the East, a church that lies in the heart of the shipping district, down the Thames from Westminster. (This church was destroyed by German bombs during the Blitz and only the tall, roofless walls remain, preserved as part of a rose-filled garden) John may have been related to the earlier Galloways, or he could have been among the many newcomers to London. The city's population, which was about 50,000 in the early 1550's, would quadruple by the end of the century as people poured in from the countryside.

A William Galloway, son of Denys, who was christened at Saint Dunstan's in 1576 may be the one who came to America; if so, he would have been forty-seven years old at the time of his voyage. This would not have been an unusual age to emigrate, as many of the Virginia adventurers were older men. The second Galloway to arrive was Richard, in 1646. He may have been the Richard, son of William Galloway, who was christened at Saint Dunstan's in 1614 and who would have been thirty when he emigrated. One reason to suppose these two men might have gone to Virginia is that they do not appear in Saint Dunstan records after the dates that they arrived in America.

Saint Dunstan's is often named in British records of the time in connection with voyages to Virginia. The customs house was located in the parish and parishioners included many shipowners and tobacco merchants. The Saint Dunstan's Galloways would have had had ample opportunity to mingle with shipowners and sailors returning from from Virginia, whose glowing, if often fanciful, reports of life in the New World would have encouraged them to emigrate.

We don't know these Galloways' social or economic status, but early emigrants were a mixed group. Admiralty records relating to the Virginia settlement mention not only gentlemen, servants, and soldiers, but practitioners of various trades including tallow chandler, soap boiler, tailor, pewterer, and embroiderer. Some were lured by the chance to break out of their restrictive trades and start new lives in a new land; some sought religious freedom and the chance to speak their minds; and some wanted to escape London's crowded conditions, pervasive crime, and poverty. Some immigrants managed to save or borrow money or sold their homes or other possessions to pay for the trip, while some went as indentured servants, contracting to pay back their fare by working for others.

Other English Galloways

These Saint Dunstan Galloways are probably the ones who first came to America, but there are other possibilities. Galloway itself had no families of that name at the time, but church records from the late 1500's and early 1600's show Galloways living in a number of English counties, with the highest concentrations of them found in Lincoln, Yorkshire and Northumberland in the North; Shropshire, Stafford and Worcester in the West; and Cambridge, Hertford, Oxford, and Buckingham in the South.

Thomas, Richard and William were the most common given

names among Galloway men at the time, which complicates positive identification of the Virginians. Two other Galloways named William, who are unlikely choices for the William who came to Virginia in 1623, were men who were christened with that name, one in Colchester in 1585 and another in Wolverhampton in 1580; they would have been 38 and 43 years of age respectively when they came to America. Another possible candidate is a Willelmus (sic.) Galloway, who was christened in Kirk Ella, near Hull, in 1580.

An undocumented note in a book by an unreliable genealogist says that the Richard who came to Virginia 1646 was mayor of Newcastle in 1643.[5] Assuming that the reference is to Newcastle-on-Tyne, this mayor might be the Richard Galloway who was born in the same county in 1594. Not only is there no documentation of this Galloway's arrival, but there were few emigrants to America from that part of England, and it is much more reasonable to assume that the first Galloways who came to America were Londoners.

Wherever they came from, the early Galloway arrivals were men of considerable ability, as well as physical endurance and unquestioned courage. Not only did they manage to survive the harrowing voyage and the harsh conditions of the early settlements, but some soon became prosperous landowners and merchants. By 1707, two Galloways, apparently brothers, each owned almost one thousand acres in Maryland, and one also had extensive shipbuilding and trade interests. Before long, some of these Galloways were wealthy enough to send their sons back to England for a gentleman's education. This rapid social and economic success implies an English background of some substance, as well as ability (and adaptability), plus a lot of luck.

Chapter 2

Coming to America

The First Arrivals

This writer's Galloway ancestry can be traced with certainty back to 1798, when Thomas Galloway (her great-great-great-great grandfather) died in Baltimore County, Maryland. Thomas had outlived his son (and our ancestor), William, but was survived by William's son Elihu, from whom our line of Galloways descends. Thomas' will shows that his wife was Mary Pocock Galloway and that Elihu, who was born in 1784, was the youngest of their six children. We know that Elihu was born in Maryland, married in Kentucky, and died in Indiana.

While this is as far back as we can go with clear documentation (and two centuries is an impressive span of time) there is persuasive evidence that these ancestors were descended from one of the first two Galloways to arrive in America more than a century and a half earlier: William, who landed in Virginia in 1623, or Richard, who came in 1646.

William and Richard Galloway arrived in Virginia just a few years after the first permanent English settlement had been established at Jamestown. By the time Americans declared their independence from England in 1776, Galloways had spread out to more than half of the thirteen colonies. Nineteen Galloway men served in America's Continental armies, enlisting from Georgia, Maryland, New York, North Carolina, Pennsylvania, South Carolina, and Virginia. By 1790, when the first federal census was taken, there were Galloways not only in those states, but in Maine and Kentucky, which, although still part of Virginia, would become a state in 1792.

The historian David Hackett Fischer wrote that, prior to the Revolution, the colonies were settled mainly by four waves of people: first, Puritans from the east of England who came to Massachusetts from 1629 to 1640; second, a migration from the south of England to Virginia from 1642 to 1675; third, a movement from the North Midlands to the Delaware Valley from 1675 to 1725; and, fourth, an influx from the Scotch-English Borders and Ulster who settled in the Appalachian back country, mostly during the half-century prior to the Revolution.[6]

History, like the people of whom it is composed, tends to be untidy and events and their makers are hard to categorize. This was certainly true of the Galloways. Careful research into many sources (and there are abundant, if not always complete, colonial tax rolls, court and church records, government and parish census records, early newspapers, personal narratives, etc.)[7], shows that most Galloway immigrants belonged to one of two groups. The first came from London to Virginia soon after Jamestown was founded: these would fit into Fischer's second wave. The next group consisted of various Galloways who came from Scotland or Ulster about the time of the American Revolution, many of whom moved inland as soon as they arrived; they would fall into Fischer's fourth wave.

But things aren't that simple. Some of the Virginia and Maryland Galloways moved north to the Delaware Valley, where they merged with what Fischer defines as his third group, immigrants from England's North Midlands. Some of the Galloways who settled in Appalachia were not part of Fisher's fourth wave, but came as part of the second wave, then migrated northward to the Pennsylvania backcountry.

Virginia Settlers

A Virginia Patent Book records that, in 1623, Sir George Yeardly, on behalf of the London Company, granted 450 acres of land to Captain William Epes for bringing over nine men, one of whom was William Galloway. William arrived that year in the ship *Anne*, along with four other men. Epes, who made repeated voyages between London and Virginia, brought over the other four men at a later time.

Twenty-three years later, in 1646, John Ashcomb was granted 250 acres in Norfolk County for bringing over twelve persons, including two Galloways: Richard and Mary, who presumably was his wife. Ashcomb had been in Virginia since at least 1639, when he was given land in Upper Norfolk. The 1646 grant does not specify whether all twelve persons arrived at the same time, nor does it name the ship that brought them. Five of the twelve newcomers were women, which was unusual in the early days. Only two of them, including Mary Galloway, had the same name as a male passenger. The others may have been intended as brides for earlier settlers, as in 1619, when some "Maides young and uncorrupt" were sent over for that purpose, or they have been transported as punishment for minor crimes, as was the heroine of *Moll Flanders*.

Land grants known as "headrights" were given to "any Adventurers or planters of what condicon or quallity soever" who brought over settlers.[8] However, others could claim the land if the grantee failed to "plant and seate" upon the land within three years. This system was intended to offset the costs of the voyage and to encourage immigration; people died almost as fast as they arrived, so a stream of new settlers was essential if the tenuous English toehold in Virginia was to become a firmly planted footstep.

The persons for whom "headrights" were granted came from all classes: tradesmen, yeomanry, gentry, and servants. Those who were indentured included persons of good family and standing in England, who simply lacked cash to pay the fare, or who were already in debt. Merchants, sea captains, and earlier settlers would often pay to bring people over. Some sea-worthy souls were persuaded to make the trip several times, so they could be counted for headrights more than once.

The land given Captain Epes for importing William was "on the Easterne shoare of the Bay of Chesepeiacke, nere unto the plantation of Accomacke;" the name Accomack was then used to refer to the entire lower part of the peninsula. Epes did not receive his "headright" until 1626, three years after William had arrived, so William may have settled elsewhere in Virginia. Epes' title, incidentally, could have been that of a ship's captain, but was probably military, since he seems to have been a long-term resident. In 1619, twelve years after the founding of Jamestown, court records show that he killed a Captain Stallenge in a "private quarrel;" duels were commonplace among the hot-tempered Virginians.

Admiralty records do not show the *Anne's* 1623 crossing, but do record some of its other trips to America. In October of 1628, the *Anne* had loaded tobacco in Virginia for the account of a London merchant.[9] In March of 1633, it returned to the customs house in St. Dunstan's in the East, after freighting from London in 1632.

A surprising number of ships, some unbelievably small to cross so great an ocean, shuttled back and forth from England; when the *Mayflower* berthed at Jamestown in 1635, its captain noted that five other ships, all from London, were already anchored there. The ships brought over settlers and supplies and returned with cargos of tobacco, the crop that bankrolled the growth of the southern colonies and that often substituted for scarce currency. They usually followed the trade winds from London to the West Indies, then headed up along the Atlantic Coast to Virginia. The typical voyage lasted three or four months, but one ill-starred crossing in 1643 is recorded as taking twenty months. Storms and wrecks were not the only risks of passage, for Spanish galleons that patrolled the southern waters might seize ships and take them to Cadiz, where the passengers would be held for ransom.

Ship owners were paid by the head for their passengers, so they crammed as many as possible into the small, dank, airless holds. The fare was scanty and often spoiled. An officer of the

Mayflower, testifying to rebut charges that passengers were underfed during a 1635 voyage to Virginia, said that every mess of five persons was allowed a quarter can of beer at each meal, and sometimes between meals when the weather was hot, plus five biscuits or, when those were gone, the equivalent in broken bread. Beef and "pease" were provided three days a week, and fish and oil on the other days.

The ship's captain, who had made six voyages to Virginia, testified that three or four of his ship's 140 passengers usually died on the crossing. Not only were people underfed, but the close quarters bred disease. When the passengers finally staggered off the ships, many were too weak to survive their first winter in Virginia.

William's New World

William, the first Galloway in America, arrived in 1623, just sixteen years after the English had founded their first permanent settlement at Jamestown and three years after the Pilgrims came ashore at Plymouth Rock. Unlike the English settlement at Roanoke Island in 1587, which we know as the "Lost Colony," the men who settled Jamestown (and the first group was composed only of men, although they were soon joined by women) not only survived, but conquered the wilderness.

The tourist who visits the Jamestown restoration today finds a cluster of tidy cabins centered around a meeting house and protected by a stockade of tall palings. Within, neatly-costumed people ply their homely crafts. Nearby is an equally tidy reconstruction of an Indian town, with people pretending to be Indians. The scene is one of industry and order, noble savages and intrepid settlers cheerfully co-existing.

The reality was very different, for the story of the early settlements is one of betrayal by Whites and Indians alike, merciless massacres and revenging raids, "starving times," wholesale disease and death, neglect by the colony's English sponsors, and constant bickering among the settlers. But out of all of this chaos and criminality, came the first permanent English settlement in the New World-- and the Galloways were part of it.

When William arrived, the colony was barely intact. The Indians, scarred by contacts with Spanish explorers, were wary of Whites and alarmed about the encroachments on their land. Clashes erupted and often proved fatal to some of the participants. Powhatan, the brilliant leader of a confederation of tribes, bided his time, plotting with his chiefs. Then, the year before William's arrival, Indian arrows and axes fell on the English settlements in an unexpected and unified attack. Only a warning by an Indian who had been converted to Christianity alerted Jamestown in time to save it from becoming another "lost colony." As it was, the raid killed almost a third of the 1,240 settlers.

English retaliation was unrelenting. Equipped with muskets and armor, the settlers waited until the Indians had brought in their harvest and then raided their towns, seized their stores of food and seed corn, and burned their huts. After several years of this attrition, the surviving Indians retreated west, ceding the peninsula to the English.

Just as the Englishmen who settled Virginia were a different breed than the Ulstermen who later swarmed into Appalachia, so the various Indian tribes had different cultures. Nor were hostilities just a matter of Whites vs. Indians: throughout these centuries, Indian tribes warred against each other, with constantly shifting alliances, just as did the European nations. The Indians around Jamestown belonged to the Algonquian tribes who had been brought into a loose confederacy under Chief Powhatan. Mostly farmers, they lived in small villages and were relatively "civilized." But they were far from peaceful. Oliver LaFarge, a perceptive student of the early Indians, comments that they "had a noble religion, a fine organization, lived comfortably, made good pottery, [and]. . . cultivated wide fields.." Still, "they called war their "beloved occupation". . . Warfare was spoken of as the greatest of delights, and it was practiced with the utmost cruelty."[10]

The year after the massacre, an epidemic carried off more settlers than had been killed in the uprising. Times were grim; during the colony's first seventeen years, six settlers died for every one who survived. They died as a result of Indian wars, disease, famine, and even crime.[11] But the fearful mortality didn't staunch the steady flow of new settlers. Even if the death rates had been known in London, many would have thought that the opportunities were worth the gamble, particularly in light of conditions in that overcrowded city. One historian commented that "It was a period of land-hunger in England. . . Unemployed craftsmen, too, could be sure that in the new settlements their skill would be in great demand."[12]

Those promoting emigration to Virginia might have lied about the dangers, but they didn't have to lie about the land itself, for it would have been hard to exaggerate its beauty and resources. The tidewater area was covered with what one settler called the "greatest pyne trees and firre trees we ever saw." The rivers spawned numerous kinds of fish. There were abundant oyster banks, while terrapin and crab were there for the taking. Otter, beaver and muskrat were plentiful, as were duck, geese and turkey. The thriving cornfields planted by Indians proved the land's potential for farming. There were, in truth, fortunes to be made for those settlers who survived.

The first settlements were crude, semi-military outposts and were peopled by a motley group. Some of them were "gentlemen adventurers," who had been advised to bring with them not only plain fare like "oates, meale and pease," but "Canary sack, marmalades, .. a good mastiffe."[13] At the other end of the social scale were servants and in between were soldiers, tradesmen, and craftspeople. When these ill-assorted folk weren't fighting Indians, they kept busy suing each other. About the time of William's arrival, court records show suits for calling someone a "roage;" for misuse of an apprentice (the court voided the indenture); and to enforce a wager that "Wm. Burdette should never match with the Widow Sanders while they lived in Virginia."[14]

Against all odds, the colony flourished. In 1649, only 26 years after William's arrival and three years after Richard's, about 29 sail arrived in the colony to trade. (When they unloaded their cargo of tobacco on the Thames-side docks the next March, they would learn that King Charles I had been executed and a Commonwealth established in England). By 1649, the population of the colony had shot up to about 15,000 English and 300 Negroes. The latter were brought in from the West Indies by New Englanders, who didn't acquire scruples about their vicious trade until the profit had gone out of it, generations later.

The William who arrived in 1623 apparently founded a line of American Galloways. A William Galloway, who was probably this man or his son, was recorded as being in Nansemond County, near Norfolk, in 1678. Richard and Mary also made their way to Nansemond, (an Indian term for "place of good fishing,") which was the site of a Puritan settlement. According to an account by one of the men who, under Captain John Smith, first explored there in 1608, the Indians greeted them with song and dance and welcomed them into their homes. But the warm welcome was a trap, for they lured the English further and further up the river, then let loose a hail of arrows. The English responded with musket fire and warned the Indians that, unless they brought corn for the settlement, their homes and canoes would be burned. The optimistic narrator wrote that they then "departed good friends."[15]

Other Virginia Galloways

Other Galloways surface in the records and then disappear, probably failing to survive the rigors of colonial life or opting to go home to England. In 1671, a servant was sent from England to Henry Galloway in Virginia and, in 1697, five men shipped from Liverpool to America, bound to Randle Galloway for terms of from four to nine years.[16] Randle was listed as being in either Virginia or Maryland, so may have been among the many people, including several Galloways, who made that move; or, he may have been a ship owner who brought servants over on consignment. He is probably the same Randle (or, in this reference, Randall) Galloway whose four children were christened in Liverpool, England, between 1680 and 1690.

Early Virginia records refer to other Galloways who might be part of our family line. In 1714, William Galloway of Northumberland County (north of Norfolk), was deposed about a will he had witnessed in 1709, which means that he was in Virginia by the earlier date;[17] since Northumberland is part of Accomack, he probably was a descendent of the William who landed almost a century earlier.

Five years later, in the same county, Alice Galloway bound her son William to Charles Lee, a Justice of the Peace, and her 5-year-old son Moses to Thomas Hubbard to be trained as a shoemaker.[18] Alice may be the widow of the earlier William and, perhaps unable to support her sons, apprenticed them to be taught a trade. The elder boy might be the same William Galloway who would witness wills in Northumberland County in 1746 and 1767.

There were a few other Galloways in Northumberland County in the Eighteenth Century. David Galloway administered estates in 1748 and 1751. In 1746, he was mentioned in Ben Franklin's *Pennsylvania Gazette*, when two men indentured to him, "Alexander Jamieson, Scotch servant, weaver by trade and John Skerum, English servant, who pretends to be a baker," stole a schooner and murdered the skipper. The Governor offered a reward of 10 pounds for capturing the men, while Galloway offered 10 pistoles for return of the schooner. In 1762, Samuel Blackwell's will left the substantial sum of "fifty pounds current money for to take care of my books and to settle my accounts with M. Galloway," and a John Galloway witnessed a 1771 will. However, this John was probably the Maryland attorney of that name, who often did business with other colonies.

Records show a few early Galloway immigrants who, fortunately for family respectability, don't seem to be part of our line. In 1635, Charles Galloway, age 19, was "transported" from

London to the Barbados, but there is no indication that he came to the mainland; Barbados' English population was roughly the same size as Virginia's, and it was considered to be a more desirable destination. In 1656, a London court ordered "John Harvey alias Gale alias Galloway" to be transported to America, but we don't know if he was even a Galloway, since this was only his third choice of names. A James Galloway was transported from London's Newgate prison to an unnamed American port in 1745; we don't know what crime he committed, but a fellow prisoner's only crime was stealing a handkerchief.[19] James may have been one of the many Jacobites who were transported that year for backing the wrong faction in a dispute over rights to the Throne.

Chapter 3

To Maryland and Beyond

After Virginia, Galloways next appear further north along the western shore of Chesapeake Bay, in Maryland's Anne Arundel County. Like other families who first settled there, they came not directly from England, but from Virginia.

William Galloway came to Virginia in 1623; Maryland land was surveyed for a William Galloway 36 years later. Richard arrived in 1646; Maryland land was surveyed for a Richard Galloway just three years later. These are almost certainly the same men or their sons; not only were there few Englishmen in America at that time, let alone ones of the same names, but the Galloways moved north as part of a religious group that fled persecution in Virginia.

The Move to Maryland

The first Galloways to arrive in America probably left England for religious reasons, as part of the Puritan rebellion. Puritans were a group who aimed at "purifying" the Church of England from the remnants of Roman Catholicism in its doctrines and practices. William Galloway left London in 1632, four years after King Charles I had appointed a new Bishop, William Laud, with a mandate to destroy Puritan power, which was centered in the city. Civil war broke out in 1642 and raged until 1645, when the King's Royalist forces were decisively defeated by Parliamentary troops under Oliver Cromwell. Richard and Mary came to America in 1646, just after the end of the civil war, when schisms developed among the victorious Puritans.

We do not know where William settled in Virginia, but it is likely that he, as well as Richard and Mary, came to Norfolk County, which then included Nansemond, to join a group of Puritans organized by a wealthy merchant of London and Amsterdam, Edward Bennett. In 1620, Bennett formed a company that sent 200 settlers to Virginia, many of whom were slaughtered in the Indian uprising two years later. He was granted 2,000 acres in Nansemond and came over himself in 1642, bringing with him members of an independent church.

Over the years, his six ships brought over hundreds more persons of his religious persuasion. Richard and Mary were probably among them, for Bennett had ties to Saint Dunstan's Parish, and the Galloways there would have been likely recruits for his settlement. William was also probably one of Bennett's imports, for he was later mentioned as being among the Namsemond group of settlers, and the ship in which he arrived, the *Anne*, was often used by Bennett to bring new groups of settlers and various goods to Virginia.

In 1643, Bennett alarmed Virginia authorities by bringing three Puritan preachers down from Boston. The colonial Assembly, understandably nervous in light of the revolt in England, quickly enacted a law forbidding any minister to officiate at a service who did not use the Church of England's Book of Common Prayer. Some of the "independent churchmen" were banished and some were even imprisoned. So Bennett's imported preachers went back to Boston and he and his fellow dissenters began to look for a safer haven.

They found it in the neighboring colony of Maryland which, in 1648, invited them to settle within its borders. Maryland had been founded in 1631, when Charles I granted a charter to the first Lord Baltimore to found a colony in America for Catholics. The expected influx of Catholics did not occur, so the colony's Proprietors decided to allow other religious groups to settle. Now, they promised land and religious freedom to Nansemond's persecuted Puritans.

From four to six hundred Nansemond settlers, led by Richard

Bennett and William Ayres, left Virginia and settled in Maryland on the banks of the Severn, near present-day Annapolis.[20] (Incidentally, Ayres' daughter married Samuel Chew, who came to Maryland in 1649; several generations of Chew's descendents would intermarry with the Galloways.[21])

In 1650, Maryland's legislature created Anne Arundel County, which included the dissenters' settlement. This was the first county created in the colony, which was still mostly wilderness and far from peaceful. In retribution for the murder of an Englishman, the same legislature directed a march on the Indians. The costs of the military action were to be met by a levy of half a bushel of corn per freeman. An order that Indians keep out of the county was not effective and, ten years later, another troop of militia was raised to proceed against them.

There was ongoing political turmoil as well, for the Proprietary authorities were concerned about the new arrivals' unorthodox tendencies. They were right to worry, for Puritans helped bring about a transfer of control from the Proprietors to Parliamentary commissioners. After the downfall of Cromwell in England, however, Lord Baltimore regained control of the province.

The Rent Rolls (early land records) serve as a reliable record of early settlers in Maryland, for all land was owned by the Proprietor and all transactions were recorded. After 1684, land could be purchased; until then, it was obtained through grants by the Proprietor, with the number of acres granted depending on factors such as the age, social status, and sex of the applicants. The grantee could sell the land, although the Proprietor actually kept title and charged a token rent; hence the term "Rent Rolls." The Conditions of Plantation allowed a person to claim a grant for transporting himself, family members, servants, and others. In 1648, a grant of 50 acres to each servant at the time he or she completed their indenture was authorized. A claimant applied to the provincial Secretary, who then ordered a survey of the land claimed, a procedure that could take time.

Richard and William Galloway were both early participants in Bennett's migration from Virginia, which began in 1649.[22] In

1650, there was a reference to William at Round Bay and, in 1651, he was recorded as owning land at Galloway's Creek; eight years later, a 100-acre tract was surveyed for him and his wife Lucy Child, who were entitled to 50 acres each because they had "completed their time of service in this Province." A year earlier, John Norwood had received fifty acres for transporting Lucy into the Province, so her "term of service" was apparently one year, presumably in return for her passage from Virginia.

The tract was named "Clinke," perhaps in reference to the sound made by a surveyor's chain, and began "at a marked Oak by a marsh." The Galloways must have been the original settlers, for the tract was described as being on the north side of "Galloway's Creek." It was located in Middle Neck Hundred, near Round Bay on the south bank of the Severn River, which runs down to Chesapeake Bay. William did not stay there long, but soon moved north to Baltimore County and, in 1667, his Anne Arundel land was sold; we will later trace his descendents, who presumably include our own ancestors.

Richard, however, stayed to found a line of Maryland Galloways. He had joined Bennett's colony in 1646, then been "transported" to Maryland in 1649, meaning that someone else paid for his passage, and his son was born in Anne Arundel County that year. In 1650, he is recorded as witnessing Richard Talbot's will, which affirms that he was part of the Quaker community. In 1657, land adjacent to William's was surveyed for Richard, beginning "at a pear tree at the head of Galloway's Creek."

The West River Quakers

Richard soon moved about 15 miles south to West River, the heart of the Puritan settlement. In 1661, 100 acres of a 600 acre parcel named "Brownton" were sold to Richard, who was described as "inhabitant of the land." Brownton was in the center of the West River community, and was where the Meeting House, the center of any Quaker community, would be built.

Richard Talbot also owned part of this land.

Richard Galloway purchased this tract, but other land at West River came to him through "gift and favor." In 1662, 250 acres, called "Galloway," were surveyed for him, consisting of 125 acres each granted to him and his wife (whose name was Hannah, although she was not identified in the grant). He named his tracts, appropriately, "the Gift" and "the Favour." In 1682, these tracts were re-surveyed and each parcel was found to be but 115 acres. "Favour" apparently was not yet cleared as farmland; in 1700, when Richard's son exchanged it for a parcel adjacent to Talbot's land, it was described as being "in the woods."

Richard, like many of the Nansemond transplants, converted to the Quaker faith, and his descendants became stalwart Friends. The Society of Friends (called Quakers because they sometimes quaked with ecstasy during spells of religious fervor) was founded in 1652 by George Fox, an English shepherd who experienced a religious vision while wandering in the fields. The Quakers pushed the Puritan argument against Popery to its limit by admitting no ordained ministers, no sacraments, and no liturgy. Their faith prohibited paying taxes or performing military service. Despite persecution by the authorities, the sect flourished in northern England and quickly spread to America.

But emigration did not end the Quakers' troubles. In Massachusetts, their missionaries were jailed and whipped by the governing Puritans, who believed that rigid regulation was necessary to control man's sinful nature. Converts to the Friendly Persuasion opposed this view, holding that God's word was revealed through an "inner light," which, if followed, would make government and armies unnecessary. Nor were they welcome in Virginia, where the 1660 Assembly passed legislation to suppress an "unreasonable and turbulent sort of people, called Quakers."

The Quakers eventually found acceptance in the mid-Atlantic colonies, where they would flourish for decades. The year after the Namsemond Puritans arrived in Maryland, the Assembly passed a law to protect all Christians' "conscience in matters of religion." This Act, the first in America to assure religious freedom, not only protected the rights of the now-outnumbered Catholics, but made members of other faiths welcome. The first Quaker missionaries arrived in Maryland less than a decade later and quickly converted most of the Nansemond Puritans to their faith.

By 1672, a meeting house had been built at West River and George Fox, the Quaker's founder, came up from Jamaica, where he was visiting, to attend its first general meeting. For several days, he preached to an overflow crowd that gathered to hear the famous man, who "expounded his doctrines with singular clearness, and with a voice remarkable for mellowness, prayed from the depths of his soul."[23]

The West River Meeting was the largest in Maryland and its members were a close-knit group. Their children intermarried, they were named as guardians and testators in each other's wills, and they often were partners in business and joined in land purchases. The Maryland Quakers held their annual meeting at West River, an event that not only set policies for all of the Colony's Quakers, but served as a social gathering and a venue for transacting business.

The Galloways were among the most prominent members of the West River Meeting. In a report on dissenters in 1672, the Sheriff of Ann Arundel County wrote that "the Quakers have one timber-work meeting house at West River. . . and have no preachers in this county but Mr. Richardson and Samuel Galloway's Wife [Ann Webb, whose husband was Richard's son]."[24]

While carrying on her ministry, "Mistress Ann," as she was called, bore eleven children, eight of whom lived to adulthood. One son was born in London, in 1689, while she was there on religious business. When she died in 1723, she was buried at London's Bunhill ("bone-hill") Fields, where George Fox and other luminaries of the faith were interred, (and which holds the dust of Blake, Bunyon, and Defoe).[25] Ann was not the only prominent Quakeress; the first "publishers of truth," as their missionaries were called, sent to America were women; despite their sex, they were jailed, stripped naked, and whipped from town to town by the Christian folk of Boston.

The Anne Arundel Quakers were not disadvantaged by their religion, for many of them prospered and became prominent in political affairs. Quakers could be fined or even imprisoned by colonial officers for refusing to train in the militia, but a way was found to accommodate their pacifism. As each male Friend reached military age, his Meeting would give him a certificate to show to the military authorities, and he was merely fined for his refusal to serve.[26]

Richard Galloway's two sons, Samuel and Richard, were among the West River Quakers who rapidly prospered. By 1707, Samuel owned nine parcels of land in Ann Arundel County, with a total of 1,400 acres. These included the home place of "Galloway," which had been surveyed for his father in 1662, and several tracts adjacent to it which he had purchased from the original grantees. The same survey showed that his brother Richard owned four parcels, with a total of almost 700 acres. Samuel's will, dated 1719, left his holdings to his five sons: Samuel, Joseph, John, Richard, and Peter.

The Anne Arundel Galloways proliferated. To the dismay of anyone trying to trace their family trees, they usually passed the same group of family names on to their sons. We have noted that the Richard who came to Maryland in 1649 had two sons, Richard and Samuel. Samuel named his sons Samuel, Joseph, John, Richard and Peter. This second Samuel named his sons Samuel, Richard, and Joseph, while his brother John named his sons Samuel, John and Joseph, and his brother Peter named his son Joseph; the other two brothers had only daughters. These names were carried on through later generations. The 1780 census of Anne Arundel County listed households headed by Benjamin, John, Joseph and Samuel.

A few other Galloways soon appear in early Anne Arundel County records; they may or may not be related to the earlier arrivals. James is listed as transported in 1677, perhaps brought in by now-established Galloway kinfolk; he apparently moved on, for the next reference to a James Galloway was in 1716, in another county. In 1704, a Thomas Galloway recorded a cattle mark: "a Cropp and two Slitts in each Ear."

In 1744, a John Galloway was transported to Kent County, and a James Galloway followed the next year, although it is not clear whether he was taken to Maryland or Virginia. Both came as "King's Passengers," or felons, although their crimes may have been political, or even nonexistent. Before the Revolution, more than 50,000 English were sent to America as felons and, after 1730, all went to Maryland or Virginia. The English used this method to clear their principal prisons on a regular basis, to suit the labor needs of American planters who exported tobacco.[27] The dates they were transported suggest that John and James Galloway were probably captured Scots, for these were the last years of the Jacobite Rebellion, which would end in 1746 with the slaughter at Culloden; almost a thousand of the Scots taken prisoner there were sold to American planters.

The Baltimore Branch

The Galloways were no sooner settled in Anne Arundel County than they began to acquire land elsewhere in the Colony, on both sides of Chesapeake Bay. In some places, they built homes and raised families; in others, they owned land but did not live there; in still others, only place names mark their presence.

In tracing various lines of Galloways, it should be noted that even reasonably reliable sources, such as public and church records, don't always agree. Not only do they vary in the spelling of names, but they often differ about dates. For example, sources may agree on the day and month of a birth, marriage, or death, but give different years for the event; for this reason, two years, separated by a slash, are sometimes given here.

While births, deaths and marriages were not always recorded, and many settlers died intestate, land records are a reliable way to track family lines, and Maryland kept careful records of wills, land transactions, tax rolls, and other legal matters. These records identify forty-seven different parcels of land owned by Galloways during the period from 1662 to 1768, located in seven counties: Anne Arundel, Baltimore, Calvert, Cecil, Dorchester, Harford, and Talbot. Almost all of these tracts can be shown to have belonged to either Richard or William's descendants.

Even without these land records, which are conclusive, the paucity of settlers and the repetitions of given names indicate that all early Maryland Galloways were related to Richard's West River Galloways, who were blessed with numerous male descendants, or to William. Until 1680, land was granted only to new settlers or by the Proprietor's favor. But, once the land was granted, there was a brisk trade in these rights and, when the headright system was done away with, newly-opened tracts could be purchased by anyone who had the money. The West River Galloways apparently had an itch to explore, and their name crops up in all of the counties that border the Chesapeake Bay. No great distances were involved in going from one county to another, and the calm waters of the Bay made travel by boat an easy alternative to the few roads available.

The 1790 census showed that, of the thirteen Galloway households in Maryland, four were still in Anne Arundel, but six were in Baltimore County, which borders it to the north, and two were in Harford and Cecil counties, which were once part of it. Cecil County, which is in the northeast corner of Maryland, was formed in 1672 and Harford, which is between Baltimore and Cecil, was formed in 1773. To further complicate matters, these counties' boundaries have shifted over the years

Baltimore County was formed in 1659, although the city was not chartered until 1729, almost eighty years later than West River. Many of its settlers came from the adjacent colonies of Pennsylvania and Virginia, but many came up from Anne Arundel. Land records have many references to Richard Bennett, who led the move there from Virginia. John Paca and Aquila Hall, good West River names, were among the winners in a 1770 election in Baltimore.

In 1667, a New England merchant sold land in Baltimore County to William Galloway, who was described as a "planter." The same year, William sold "Clinke" in Anne Arundel County, which he had been granted in 1651. He died soon after moving north, for a 1673 survey referred to 100 acres in Baltimore County's Gunpowder River Hundred that were "possessed by James Durham for William Galloway's orphans." Durham had married William's widow, Margaret Enloe. One of Maryland's Quaker Meetings was located in Gunpowder Hundred, so William may have part of a group who were moving up from West River. "Hundreds" were geographical divisions that served as voting districts and as military units for men able to bear arms. William did not stay there long,

Two years later, one of these orphans, also named William, was recorded as appraising estates in Cecil County, which had been created in 1674 from Baltimore and Kent Counties, at the uppermost tip of Chesapeake Bay. The area was far from peaceful for, a few years before William arrived, Indians had plundered Robert Gorsuch's cabin at Gunpowder River and killed his wife, then returned a few days later to kill his cows. In 1682, vengeful settlers captured twenty-five warriors and burned them alive. As if this violence weren't enough, there were threats of war with Dutch families who were settling in the area.[28]

By 1684, William owned "Galloway's Farm" and "Galloway's Choice," with a total of 486 acres, in Cecil County. In 1692, fifty more acres were sold to William for 7,200 pounds of tobacco; tobacco was often used as currency, since British money was scarce and the Colonies were not allowed to issue their own. William was described as being "of Gunpowder River," confirming that he was one of the orphans who inherited land there.

In January of 1700, his son William sold "Galloway's Farm," which amounted to 286 acres, and which he had acquired from his father. The next year, the senior William deeded all of his remaining property in Cecil County to his daughter Hannah and her husband, because he was moving, perhaps back to Baltimore

County; in return, they agreed to maintain him "with food, drink, apparel, lodging and necessary phisiche during his natural life." The wife of Richard Galloway who arrived in Maryland about the same time as William was named Hannah, and the fact that William gave this name to his daughter implies that they were related.

William was still alive in 1705, when he was named in the will of his son, who was also named William, and who left a wife named Margaret and sons named William and Henry. The latter William married Priscilla Carr in 1725. Baltimore County Records not only show that he sold a tract of land in 1708, but that he witnessed a will in 1714 and a deed in 1726. He died in 1743, leaving his property to his wife, Priscilla, and their children, whose story we shall pick up later.

The West River Connection

Throughout the early years, records show many transactions in Baltimore/Harford/Cecil Counties involving Galloways who bought land there but remained residents of West River. As early as 1747, for example, Samuel Galloway of West River offered land for sale in Baltimore County. His son Joseph, described as being "of Anne Arundel" had bought 1,500 acres there in 1726, and bought 305 more in 1750. In 1737, a "coffee man" of London sold 300 acres in Baltimore County to John Galloway, another of Samuel's sons and a prominent West River attorney. In 1742, John held power of attorney for another English owner in the purchase of a tract which he later bought for himself, and which his heirs sold when he died in 1747. When Samuel died in 1719, his eldest son, Samuel, was already settled in Calvert County.

The fact that there were four Meeting houses in Baltimore County shows that many of the settlers were original settlers from Anne Arundel County or their descendants. In 1728, Samuel Galloway's son Richard married Mary Paca, daughter of Aquila Paca, at the Bush River Meeting House, located in what was then Baltimore (but would become Harford) County. They returned to the West River plantation he had inherited from his father, where he died two years later.

There were other Galloways listed in early Baltimore/Cecil County records. In 1716, James, listed as a planter of Cecil County, bought 66 acres. In 1729, Peter and John Galloway witnessed a will (although this does not mean that they lived in the county) and John's heirs were listed in 1754 as owning 1,800 acres on the Gunpowder River. In 1733, Moses bought land in the county. Four years later, Richard was on the tax list.

There were also other references to a William Galloway, for he and George served on a jury in 1737. A tax list that year showed William as owning two slaves, and he is elsewhere recorded as receiving a bounty for "squirrill's heads." Baltimore county tax records for 1762 refer to Joseph Galloway's heirs and to a Samuel Galloway. In 1768, signers of a petition to move the county seat to Baltimore included Aquila, Moses, Thomas, and William Galloway.

Galloways bought land across the Bay from West River and Baltimore. In 1659, the year that Richard Galloway received his original grant in Anne Arundel County, the Rent Rolls of Dorchester County, which is on Maryland's Eastern Shore, showed Richard as owning a 700 acre tract called "Barren Island;" he acquired this by marrying the widow of the original grantee's son. While he held the land until his death, there is no indication that he left West River to live there.

The first U.S. Census, taken in 1790, showed thirteen Galloway households in Maryland, almost all headed by familiar family names: John, Joseph, Samuel and Benjamin in Anne Arundel county; Aquila, John, Thomas, William, James and Mary in Baltimore; John in Cecil; Absalom in Harford; and Samuel in Montgomery. Available records support the assumption that all these Galloways were related and were descended from those who came to West River in 1650. Despite this flourishing start, the 1810 census found only four Galloway households left in the state, all located in Baltimore and Harford counties. As we shall see, some Galloways had moved on to new frontiers.

In addition to land owned by the Galloways, a number of references to land named "Galloway" are found in the wills of other people, indicating that a member of the family had been one of the early arrivals at the place in question and a site had been named after him. These include a 1675 will in St. Mary's County, to the south; a 1684 will across the Bay in Talbot County; and a 1680 will in Somerset County, just above the Virginia line. Various records show parcels of land named not only Galloway and Galloway's Farm, but Galloway's Point, Fancy, Choice, Chance and Enlargement.

Manors, Manners and Marriages

Samuel Galloway, of West River, grandson of the first Richard, left numerous manors when he died in 1719, so that each of his five sons inherited a substantial estate. The eldest, also named Samuel, was left land in Calvert County, "where he is now seated;" when he died three years later, his plantation was divided among his three sons. The 1719 will left the home place, "Galloway," to the second son, Joseph, along with parts of other plantations. Another of the elder Samuel's estates was divided between his sons John and Richard, with an additional manor left to Richard. John later added to his holdings, and had 2,000 acres at the time of his death. The fifth son, Peter, was left a manor which he sold a few years later when he moved to the lower counties of Pennsylvania, which later became Delaware.

The Galloways, especially the West River branch, married (and inter-married) into prominent Maryland families, including the Chews, Pacas, Pembertons, Talbots, and Richardsons. Like the Galloways, most of these families had come up from Virginia with Bennett and become Quakers.

The children of the Samuel Galloway whose will was cited above are prime examples. Samuel's daughter Mary married Dr. Samuel Chew, the grandson of the Samuel Chew who came to Virginia in 1624 and who moved to Maryland about the same time as the Galloways. When Mary (Galloway) died, Dr. Chew married Mary (Paca) Galloway, widow of his brother-in-law Richard. Mary and Richard Galloway's brother Joseph, meanwhile, had married and produced a daughter, Mary, who married her cousin (Dr. Chew's son), Benjamin. Benjamin and Mary (Galloway) Chew's daughter Mary then followed family tradition by marrying her cousin, John Galloway.[29]

The branches on the family tree were further entangled when Joseph Galloway, who inherited the family homestead from his father, married Susannah Paca, whose sister Mary had married his brother Richard (and who subsequently, as we have seen, married her brother-in-law Dr. Chew).

The remaining Galloway brother, Peter, did not choose a Chew or a Paca, but married his cousin Elizabeth Rigbie, whose mother was a Galloway. Inbreeding was commonplace in those times, especially in a relatively isolated Quaker community like West River, whose members were not allowed to marry outside their faith. The practice obviously didn't injure the family intellect, for Peter's son was one of the leading lawyers and politicians of his time and Benjamin Chew capped a brilliant career by becoming Chief Justice of Pennsylvania.

Some of the West River Galloways, like many of their fellow Quakers, were not only planters, but showed a talent for business. Samuel Galloway, great-grandson of the Richard who arrived in 1649 and grandson of the Samuel whose wife was a Quaker preacher, was the wealthiest of the Maryland Galloways. In 1755, he bought a plantation from the Talbots, to whom it had been patented in 1659. He renamed it "Tulip Hill" and built an imposing mansion there; in fact, he built it so well that it still stands, the handmade brick now mellowed to a soft rose color. It has been praised as one of Maryland's finest early homes, "standing in a grove of ancient tulip poplars and on a lovely rise of land which together gave the house its name. . . looking out from its terraced hilltop over almost a mile of farmland to the Chesapeake Bay."[30] The estate, which his son John inherited , had extensive orchards and a famous stable of racing horses.

Samuel's wife Anne Chew died in childbirth before the house was completed. He never remarried, but his hospitality was enjoyed by many, especially prominent horsemen including George Washington. The Maryland *Gazette* once reported that he entertained an English gentleman who came to the colonies "to take his diversion in a tour;" unfortunately, the visitor died while at Tulip Hill. Galloway kept close ties to England, making several trips there, where he not only transacted business but enjoyed socializing at his favorite clubs and coffeehouses.

Samuel's great wealth reflects Annapolis' position as a center of shipping trade with both old and New England. Not only did Samuel own substantial tracts of land, some inherited, but he had a fleet of ships, including the *The Swallow, the Dragon* and *the Grove*, many of which were built in his own shipyard, using the great oaks that grew in the area. Planters shipped tobacco and grain to be sold in England, then used much of the proceeds to buy commodities that were not available at home, allowing the ship owner to profit from both legs of the voyage.

The shipping business carried risks other than the normal ones of storms at sea. Hostile ships roamed the Atlantic, and one of Galloway's ships was seized by French privateers while *en route* to Barbados. Galloway used one of his own fast ships for smuggling sugar from the French Indies in defiance of the British Trade Acts and, in 1757, advertised for crew to man a privateer of his that mounted 18 guns.

One of the commodities Galloway imported was indentured servants, whom he then sold into service to pay for their passage. At the end of the term of indenture, they were legally entitled to land, clothing and equipment so they could start out on their own. Galloway kept some of these servants for himself, but not always profitably; several of them, including two ships' carpenters, abrogated their contracts by running away, probably escaping to the anonymity of the frontier.

For a time, Galloway also engaged in the slave trade, importing some directly from Angola. This venture did not prove profitable and was soon abandoned; after being specially fitted for slaves, the ships were unsuited for other cargo.[31]

Quakers may have been troubled by the institution of slavery, but they were slow to take action against it. In Philadelphia, the heart of Quakerism, the Yearly Meeting, which set policy for local Meetings, expressed concern about slavery as early as 1758, but it was not until 1780 that the Pennsylvania Assembly abolished the practice, and it continued in Maryland until the Civil War. The British government repeatedly blocked the Pennsylvania Assembly's efforts to curb the importation of slaves, because they were viewed as property that could be used to help secure the debts that most planters owed to English traders.

Several Galloways were slave owners. A 1776 census of Anne Arundel County showed Samuel Galloway as owning seventeen slaves, and a 1737 tax list showed William Galloway owning two slaves in Baltimore County. In the 1790 census, Joseph and John of Ann Arundel County were listed as owning 41 and 50 slaves, respectively. A 1774 list of taxables in Harford County included Elizabeth Galloway, described as a free Mulatto, and Benjamin, age six, who was presumably her son; she had probably taken the name of her former owner. Her husband may have been the Benjamin Galloway who was sentenced to death for burglary in 1769, just across the Bay in what is now Delaware.[32]

Samuel Galloway and his circle lived well. He remained a Quaker, but the Meeting's influence against frivolity had clearly weakened, for an English visitor wrote of Maryland's racing season that "there are few meetings in England better attended, or where more capital horses are exhibited," and noted that the company at the evening amusements after the races had "a fashionable and brilliant appearance."[33] Planters like Samuel imported fine horses from England, attracting horse lovers including George Washington to his famous stables.

A 1763 inventory of an estate administered by Samuel's son Peter reflects the luxurious life that many planters enjoyed, for it included 53 slaves, a silver hilted sword, silver spurs, gold-studded cuff links, 12 gallons of Lisbon wine, 2 gallons of port,

48 gallons of rum, a violin, and a backgammon table.[34]

Samuel sent at least one son to Eton, where the sons of English aristocrats were educated, and where the boy acquired some less than desirable ways. In 1770, George Washington sent his step-son, Jacky Custis, to study with a clergyman in Annapolis, warning that "the time of Life he is now advancing into requires the most friendly aid and Council, especially in such a place as Annapolis." The clergyman later wrote that Jacky was too much under the influence of a "wild, volatile, idle & goodnatured" son of Mr. Samuel Galloway, adding that, "You cannot conceive with what delight Custis w'd listen to his droll Tales & Acct's of his Pranks at School in England." To make matters even worse, Galloway had a sister "young and pretty," to whom Custis paid "particular attention, exceeding bare civility."[35] (Custis ended up as a n'er-do-well, while Galloway returned to England to read law at Lincoln's Inn, then returned to Maryland, serving as its first Attorney General after statehood.)

While the West River Meeting flourished for many years, the Quakers' rigid doctrines led to defections and, eventually, a sharp decline in their numbers. Minutes of Meetings record members being disowned for "attending places of diversion, dancing, and neglecting attendance at meetings;" "being concerned with horse racing and making use of unbecoming language;" and "drinking spirituous liquor to excess."[36] But the most common cause for expulsion was for "marriage accomplished contrary to the good order." The family of the famous Pennsylvania frontiersman, Daniel Boone, left the meeting when his father was expelled for allowing his daughter to wed a non-Quaker. Many others defected when the Quaker's strict pacifism came up against the realities of defense.

Some converted to the Presbyterian Church, which had much in common with the Quakers, including self-government and rejection of most ritual, while others, including some Galloways, returned to the Church of England, once the bitter divisions caused by the Puritan revolt had faded, and still others joined one of the many offshoots of that church. Some Meetings tried to hold on to members by relaxing their standards of what was considered seemly behavior. Ann Galloway, namesake of the preacher Ann, married Joseph Pemberton, scion of another prominent Quaker family, in 1767. Despite being Quakers, the Pembertons were leaders of Philadelphia society who participated in the dancing Assemblies, and whose portraits show that they abandoned plain dress in favor of very elegant and costly apparel.

We have traced these Galloways from Scotland to London, then across the Atlantic to Virginia, and on to Maryland; now, we will go west to Pennsylvania and the Appalachian frontier. This is a digression in terms of tracking the writer's direct ancestors, for they apparently never moved to Pennsylvania. But the evidence indicates that they were related to at least some of the Galloways who settled that area, and whom they would later join in Kentucky.

Chapter 4

The Pennsylvania Frontier

The Early Arrivals

Pennsylvania's Cumberland Valley, which includes the town of Carlisle, was the center of Scotch-Irish settlement on the frontier and the place from which these intrepid people spread out across America. The fertile valley, which lies between the Susquehanna River and the Allegheny Mountains, was "the seed-plot and nursery of their race, the original reservoir which, after having been filled to overflowing, sent forth a constant stream of emigrants to the northward and especially to the South and West."[37] However, not all of these frontiersmen came directly from Ulster; many of them, including some Galloways, came from nearby areas of Pennsylvania and Maryland.

The first reliable record of Galloways in Pennsylvania is in a letter from Richard Peters, secretary of the Province, to the Governor, dated July 2, 1750. In 1740 or 1741, three or four Germans (later called Pennsylvania Dutch), had settled on the Big Juniata River. Some Delaware Indians protested to the government "with particular warmth" that this intrusion violated treaties between the Proprietor of the Province, William Penn, and the Indian confederation of Six Nations.[38] One chief explained to the Governor's Council that the Dutchmen "claimed a right to the land merely because they gave a little victuals to our warriors, who stand very often in need of it."

By a Proclamation of 1742, the Proprietors had forbidden any settlements on these lands, declaring that:

No warrant has been issued for settling of any Lands. . . west of the *Endless* or *Blue* Mountains , so that all such as have presum'd to possess themselves of any Lands there are manifest Intruders; and, as such, liable by the Laws to be removed, and, in Case of refusal, to be committed to Prison and Severely Fined.[39]

In response to the Indians' continued protest, the Governor ordered Secretary Peters to have the trespassers removed. Peters did so in June of 1743, but the determined squatters returned. In 1748, officials were sent again to warn them, but the intruders still did not leave.

The Governor was particularly anxious to preserve the alliance with the Indians because the French were threatening the frontier and enlisting Indian aid. In early 1750, he ordered Peters to go west and see that the trespassers were brought to justice. Peters reported back that, on May 22, six justices of the peace and the undersheriff of Cumberland County went to a settlement at Big Juniata, situated about ten miles north of the Blue Hill, "a place much esteemed by the Indians as some of their best hunting-grounds."

There they found five log cabins, possessed by William White, George Cahoon, David Huddleston, Andrew Lycon, and one shared by George and William Galloway. When asked by what authority they had possessed themselves of the land and erected cabins thereon, the settlers replied that they had no right, and knew that they were in contempt of the Proclamation, but they asked for mercy. White, Cahoon and Huddleston were then taken into custody, but the two Galloways showed their independence of their Scottish ancestors by running off, calling back to the authorities that "you may take our Lands and Houses and do what you please with them; we deliver them to you with all our hearts, but we will not be carried to jail."

The justices returned the next day and White, Huddleston and Cahoon posted bonds in the substantial sum of five hundred pounds each and turned their cabins over to the authorities. The officials went on to the Galloways' cabin, where they found that the occupants had left and taken all their goods with them. When the officials came back the next day, the Galloways were still gone and Lycomb, who warned them off with a gun, was taken into custody.

Peters and the magistrates agreed that "if some Cabbins were not destroyed, they would tempt the trespassers to return again, or encourage others to come there should these trespassers go away... [and] if all the Cabins were left standing, the Indians would conceive such a contemptible Opinion of the Government, that they would come themselves, in Winter, murder the People, and set their houses on fire." On these considerations, the cabins of the resisters, the Galloways and Lycomb, were burned down. Peters noted that the cabins were of no great value, but "such as the country people erect in a day or two, and cost only the charge of an entertainment," referring to the custom by which settlers would help a newcomer erect a cabin, with the host providing food and drink.

The authorities went on to other illegal settlements, where more trespassers were put under bond and a few more cabins were destroyed. This whole operation was somewhat devious and was merely designed to placate the Indians. In fact, the government had already agreed to purchase these lands and open them to settlement, and promised those persons who gave up their cabins peacefully that they could return as soon as the land purchase was completed. When the area was opened in 1755, White, Cahoon and Lycon took out warrants for land on the Juniata. The Galloways obviously were not welcome to return, but they did resettle at Great Cove, where Elizabeth Galloway would be killed in a 1755 Indian raid.

The Path to Pennsylvania

We cannot prove when or from where these Galloways came to the Juniata Valley, but it seems clear that they moved up from Maryland. A history of the Valley cited earlier says that

Marylanders were among its first settlers, and the Provincial
Secretary, Richard Peters, reported that, in 1741-42. settlers from
Maryland and other parts of Pennsylvania "stole into" the Great
Cove, which was where Galloways were later recorded as
settling.

As we know, Galloways were among the earliest settlers of
Maryland's northern counties and, by 1740, they had proliferated
in the area. Both Baltimore and West River, which were well-
stocked with Galloways, carried on a thriving trade with the
frontier, so there was constant travel back and forth between
Maryland and the Pennsylvania frontier. In 1761, Edward
Shippen of Lancaster mentioned that the Secretary of the
Province was at York, "settling accounts with Mr. Galloway,"[40]
which sounds as if that Galloway were a prominent man on the
frontier. (Shippen's brother married Jane Galloway, of Tulip Hill,
showing the ties between West River and western Pennsylvania).
Furthermore, the borders between Maryland and Pennsylvania
were not firmly fixed. During the 1730's, the Penn family held
out special inducements to persuade settlers to occupy the lands
along the border in order to prevent encroachments by
Marylanders.

Our ancestor Thomas Galloway and his son William lived
along the Gunpowder River in Maryland, about twenty miles
from the Pennsylvania border. Not only does this river originate
in Pennsylvania, but one of the earliest roads in Maryland went
north to York, coming within a few miles of the Galloways' land.
So the early Pennsylvania Galloways were geographically very
close to the Gunpowder River Galloways, making it highly
probable that they were related.

Another reason to conclude that the Maryland and
Pennsylvania Galloways were kin is that they shared many of the
same given names. There are various Maryland references to
George and William Galloway, which are the names of the men
who were evicted from their Pennsylvania cabin in 1750. George
was recorded as serving on a Baltimore County jury in 1737 but
was not mentioned again in Maryland records. Several William

Galloways appear in records of Baltimore, Harford, and Cecil counties about that time, and one of them was probably George's cabinmate.

Some of the Maryland Galloways were Quakers, while most frontier Galloways were not, but defections from that faith were common. Some of the Maryland Galloways were wealthy and educated, while most frontiersmen were not, but one frontier-reared Galloway, James, left a well-written memoir which included a Latin phrase; although this was dictated to a relative, the author must have been educated.

Most Baltimore county Galloways had only small land holdings and some might have decided to try their luck elsewhere. The move north would not have meant much change in their condition; when Galloways first appeared on the Pennsylvania frontier in 1740, northern Maryland was barely settled, so they would just be moving somewhat deeper into the wilderness if they decided to go to Pennsylvania.

At this point, a red herring needs to be buried. Some years ago, an enthusiastic but unskilled genealogist, Ruth DeVerter, published a history of her "pioneer ancestors" in which she wrote that the first Galloways in America were "seven stalwart Galloway brothers" (Samuel, John, William, James, Peter, Thomas, and George), who came from Scotland about 1740 with their mother Elizabeth and that four of them settled in Mifflin County, Pennsylvania. This "seven brothers" story has gained widespread currency, but there is no evidence to support it.

Deverter gives as her sources two books by amateur genealogists: Roy Stevenson King's *The Ancestral Pilgrimage Along Life's Pathway* and a *History of the Covenanters* by Reverend Robert Simpson.[41] King claims that the brothers arrived early in the 18th Century, probably through Philadelphia, and were the first Galloways in America; actually, Galloways had arrived more than a century earlier. He also makes the odd claim that they emigrated to County Antrim in Ireland "during the persecutions of the Christians in Scotland."

DeVerter quotes her other source, Reverend. Simpson, as

saying that "sturdier Covenanters existed not than the seven stalwart Galloway brothers of medium size with broad shoulders and sandy hair." Covenanters were Scots Presbyterians who pledged to maintain their form of worship. They supported Cromwell's rebellion, so were persecuted after 1660, when the Monarchy was restored, until 1685, when their church was again made lawful. Aside from the fact that Simpson could have no idea what these mythical brothers looked like, they would not have needed to flee Scotland for religious reasons in 1740.[42]

The facts simply do not support this story, however appealing it might seem: there are no records of seven Galloway brothers leaving the British Isles or arriving in America, although such records were carefully kept and are readily available. For example, over a thousand Scots who fought in the Jacobite Revolt of 1745 were captured, shipped and sold as indentured servants at the Maryland docks, but the roster of names does not include any Galloways, nor do several shipments in 1716. As noted earlier, a John Galloway came over in 1744 and a James in 1745, but they do not appear to be brothers, for they sailed at different dates from different ports.

Perhaps new documents will be uncovered, or some intrepid researcher will be able to make more sense out of existing clues, so that pieces of the puzzle will snap firmly into place. Until then, overwhelming evidence argues that the Pennsylvania Galloways came not from far away Scotland or Ulster, but from a few miles south in Maryland.

The 1750's: The Frontier on Fire

Pennsylvania frontiersmen clashed with the Quaker-controlled Provincial government on how to deal with the Indians. The Quakers tried to adhere to their carefully-negotiated treaties with the tribes, while most frontiersmen were Presbyterian Scotch-Irish who looked on the Indians as savages with no right to land or even to life. Secretary Peters wrote in 1730 that "The Indians are alarmed at the swarms of strangers [Ulstermen], and we are afraid of a breach between them- for the Irish are very rough to them." In another letter, he added that "the settlement of five families from Ireland gives me more trouble than fifty of any other people. Before we were broke in upon, ancient Friends and first settlers lived happily; but now the case is quite altered."[43]

By 1751, there were about 5,000 settlers in the Cumberland Valley, their presence serving to foment clashes with the Indians, who often retaliated with raids. Year after year, the Pennsylvania Assembly debated defense issues, but failed to take any action. In 1754, these hostilities exploded into war and the Indians, backed by the French, brought death and destruction to the settlements. The *Pennsylvania Gazette* of November 13, 1755, reported an Indian attack on Great Cove, just north of the Maryland border, in which seven settlers were murdered, among them Elizabeth Galloway. Three men's wives and children were missing, presumably taken captive. Another man and his wife were taken prisoner and their son was killed and scalped.[44] James Galloway, who was five at the time of the massacre, later reminisced about "seeing a horse come in all bloody, shot through the neck, and its rider killed".

About 10 miles north of Great Cove, in Fort Littleton, a settler named Johnson Elliott would have been alarmed by news of the massacre. He was an Ulsterman, for his parents, Thomas and Mary Johnston Elliott, had come to Pennsylvania from County Fermanagh in Ireland. Johnson would stay near Great Cove for the rest of his life, ending his days in Burnt Cabins. His son William, who was three at the time of the massacre, would be commissioned an ensign in the Pennsylvania militia in 1778 and would later father a girl who, in 1811, would marry Elihu Galloway.

The 1750's were desperate times on the frontier. In 1754, the British General Braddock's campaign against the French and Indians ended in ambush, forcing those of his men who weren't killed to beat a hasty retreat. The Indians, with help from the French, then carried on a devastating campaign of murder, scalping, and burning, so that by the time winter came, "all the outlying frontier settlers and their families had been killed or sent flying eastward to seek refuge in the settlements."[45]

In 1755, the Provincial land office granted thirty-three warrants for land in the newly-opened area, but Indian raids not only kept the new grantees out, but forced the forty-odd families already settled there to flee back to safer settlements.

James Galloway was born in 1750 in Lancaster County. At the age of 88, he dictated his reminiscences, relating how his family retreated to the town of York after the Indian attack on Great Cove. They stayed there two winters, and "thence removed to Loudon County, Virginia, near Leesburg, lived there at the time George III was proclaimed King, in 1760, and thence moved back to Conocogeague, in Cumberland County, Pennsylvania."[46] Leesburg is on the Maryland County line, about 30 miles from Baltimore, which again supports the theory of a Pennsylvania-Maryland tie.

The end of the French and Indian War restored some degree of stability to the frontier. By 1760, about twenty settlers had ventured back to the valley and more soon followed. Among them was George Galloway, who took out a warrant for 150 acres of land in 1766, on the south side of the Juniata River. In l767, he was listed on the tax rolls as the owner of 300 acres and, in the year 1778, he was taxed in Mifflin County as owning 148 acres, 4 horses, and 3 cattle. He remained in the county until his death in 1783.

His sons Samuel and Joseph also acquired land there, but Joseph eventually sold his to Samuel Wharton, who owned the adjoining property. Wharton was a Quaker merchant who speculated in western lands; a Philadelphian, he was a close friend of Joseph Galloway, the prominent Philadelphia politician and Loyalist leader who was descended from the West River Galloways, and who often backed Wharton's purchases of western land. As we shall see, some of this George Galloway's sons would soon move south to a new frontier in the "dark and bloody land" of Kentucky, where they would be among the first settlers.

Arrivals from Ulster

From 1750 to when the Revolution broke out in 1776, thus calling a temporary halt to immigration, shiploads of families poured into Philadelphia from Scottish settlements in northern Ireland, known collectively as Ulster. Many came by way of Dumfries, Straener, and other ports in Southwest Scotland (which is the area called Galloway), which were just across a narrow sea from Ulster. Among these immigrants were some Galloways, although there is no reason to think that they were part of our family line.

This influx of settlers included two John Galloways. One was a 25-year-old weaver, who arrived in the ship *Sally* in 1774; there are several later references to a prosperous Philadelphia tailor of the same name, who was probably the same man. The other John was a joiner who, accompanied by his wife Sara, came from Stranen to New York the same year.[47] A list of Revolutionary War pensioners includes two other Ulster-born Galloways: Peter, who was born in 1757 and enlisted from South Carolina and James, who was born a year later and enlisted from Chester County, Pennsylvania.

Ships' masters were required to record their passengers' reasons for leaving Scotland. Both of these Galloways gave "want of employment" as the cause of their move and most fellow emigrants shared this motive. They are recorded as giving such explanations as "hope to do better," and "cannot get bread in this country." One optimistic soul declared that he was leaving "to make a fortune." The master of the ship *Clementina* of Philadelphia, which brought over 90 men, 68 women and 54 children on one voyage, saved time simply writing that "all emigrated in hope of procuring a better livelihood."

There were exceptions, including emigrants who left "because others are leaving;" "cannot get a husband;" "curiosity;" and "having run away with a young widow and left a wicked wife thought shame to appear." A few of the emigrants were farmers, but most listed trades such as baker, weaver, mason and shoemaker.[48] Some chose to remain in Philadelphia, where they were quickly absorbed into the city's robust economy, but most chose to go on west, to the freedom of the frontier.

Chapter 6

Revolution: Two Sides to the Story

Our Revolution is usually viewed, at least in this country, as a struggle of American patriots against British tyrants. The truth is very different, for this was, to a great extent a civil war. At the start of the war, about a third of Americans were in favor of independence, a third were loyalists, and a third were neutral. Like the rest of the country, the Galloways were divided. While many joined Washington's army to fight for independence, a few actively supported the British. In fact, the most prominent of all American Galloways was a leading loyalist.

The Patriots

In the fateful year of 1776, an officer came to Pennsylvania's Cumberland County to raise volunteers for the newly-formed Continental Army. George Galloway's son James, age 26 and just back from an extended foray into the Kentucky wilderness, was reaping grain along with about twenty men at his father's farm. According to an account that James dictated in his old age, he told the officer that he would join up, but first had to finish harvesting the field. The officer pitched in to help and, the next morning, James shouldered his long Kentucky rifle and headed north with the recruiter.

Most frontiersmen welcomed the chance to fight against the English. They enlisted in great numbers and stayed with General Washington when more moderate colonists began to question the cost of independence and to desert the cause. In some western Pennsylvania counties, women and old men brought in the harvest, because all able-bodied men were off in the army. Not only were the frontiersmen anti-British, but they had another agenda: this was a chance to topple the Quaker oligarchy which had governed the Province since its founding.

James joined the army in July, about two weeks before the Battle of Long Island. This was a dark hour for the American cause, for Washington's army of 20,000 new recruits was no match for the more than 32,000 well-trained and well-equipped British and Hessians who had been sent to put down the rebellion. After six days of hard fighting, Washington pulled his half-starved and exhausted troops back across the river to Manhattan. The retreat was completed under cover of darkness and the demoralized men waited, short of supplies and food, while the war stagnated. James was not on Long Island during the battle, but was stationed across the river on Paulus's Hook as part of a battery that fired at British ships going up the Hudson.

After two months of duty, he made the long journey home, then re-enlisted and was back north in time for the Battle of Trenton on Christmas Day. The details of that battle may have been forgotten, but everyone remembers the often-reproduced painting of Washington and his ragged troops crossing the icy Delaware River. This desperate gamble to save the rebels' failing cause gave the colonists their first victory. The "rabble in arms" triumphed over the Hessians, crack troops hired by the English, without losing a single American life; James' Revolutionary War pension record recalls his seeing 900 Hessian soldiers who had been captured.

Enlistments in the Continental Army were for a short duration, so James left the Army briefly several times, coming back to rejoin Washington's forces. In 1778 he left the army for the last time and returned to the Pennsylvania frontier.

James was not the only one of our Galloways to take up arms. In 1776, in Maryland's Anne Arundel County, the Council of Safety commissioned John Galloway as Second Major of the South River Battalion of Militia. Another West River Galloway, Joseph, was commissioned as a Major of the South River Militia battalion by Maryland's Council of Safety, which functioned as a provisional government; he had obviously broken with his Quaker roots by taking up arms. In Baltimore County, William Galloway was commissioned as an ensign in the militia.

In all, the Daughters of the American Revolution's zealously-researched records show that nineteen Galloway men fought in the Continental Army, including not only the Marylanders just listed and all of the brothers from the Juaniata Valley settlement, but Galloways from Georgia, New York, North and South Carolina and Virginia (which then included Kentucky).[49]

The Loyalists

While nineteen Galloways served in the Continental Army, some others not only remained loyal to the British, but actively opposed revolution. The most famous (or infamous, depending on one's point of view) Galloway in American history was Joseph, who was not only opposed revolution, but was one of the most prominent and influential Loyalists. Although he was not a direct ancestor of ours, he was (if our theories are correct), part of our line of Galloways; in any event, he is a fascinating man whose life shows a forgotten chapter of the Nation's past.[50]

Joseph was born in 1730 at West River. His father was Peter (the youngest son of Samuel of Tulip Hill), who had married Elizabeth Rigbie at the Meeting House in West River, where her grandfather had acquired a 400-acre tract in 1659. Elizabeth's mother was a Galloway, so Joseph inherited a double share of the family genes. The genes, the land and the family background helped propel him on a meteoric career. His father had moved to Kent County, in the "lower counties" of Pennsylvania (now Delaware) by 1742, but young Joseph was drawn to city life and the study of law, so moved to Philadelphia. At the age of 19, he was pleading cases before the Pennsylvania Supreme Court. His specialty was property law, a subject dear to the hearts of the merchants and ship owners who ran the Province, and his practice flourished.

Philadelphia was laid out by the Quaker William Penn in 1682 and raised out of the wilderness with startling speed. By the time Joseph moved there in the 1750's, it was a city of 20,000; by the 1770's, the population had doubled, making it the largest city in the Colonies. Not only did the Quakers tolerate other religions and cultures, but their commitment to public service put the city far ahead of others in such matters as public safety and welfare.

Joseph enhanced his already brilliant prospects by marrying Grace Growden, the daughter and heir of a prominent office holder, Joseph Growden. Growden's father had come to Pennsylvania from Cornwall in southwest England in 1681, after buying 10,000 acres from William Penn. His son Joseph Growden was not only a notable landowner, but owned the largest ironworks in the colonies.

At age 25, Galloway was elected to the Pennsylvania Assembly, which was the most powerful legislative body in the colonies. Ben Franklin, then an influential legislator, jump-started the newcomer's career; the upwardly-mobile Franklin appreciated Galloway's social position as well as his brilliant mind and boundless energy. They formed a political partnership that dominated the colony up until the Revolution, working to weaken Proprietory control while resisting the rising influence of the frontiersmen.

Franklin's role was largely *in absentia*, as he left for England soon after Galloway joined the Assembly, and remained there until the Revolution. Galloway then dominated the unicameral Assembly for almost two decades, much of that time as Speaker. Reared as a Quaker, he managed to retain that group's decisive support, although he had left the Meeting, probably on the issue of pacifism.

As Speaker, he headed Pennsylvania's delegation to the First Continental Congress, where he proposed a Plan of Union with England that would have given the colonies a status similar to that later enjoyed by Canada. The plan was defeated by one vote, then expunged from the record so that Congress would appear united. Appalled by the rush to revolution, Galloway declined to serve in the Second Congress. Like most of the Philadelphia merchants whom he had represented for so long, he believed that America's grievances should be redressed, but not at the cost of rebellion. As violence replaced order in the Province, he barely escaped lynch mobs and was forced to flee north to seek protection from the advancing British army.

Welcomed by the British as the most prominent Loyalist still in America, after most had fled or been imprisoned, Galloway furnished intelligence to the high command. His assurances that most people in the "Middle Colonies" were loyal helped to persuade the British commander, Sir William Howe, to march on Philadelphia. Galloway was subsequently named civil superintendent of the occupied city and made responsible not only for keeping order, but for procuring supplies, regulating shipping, and a host of other duties. He also raised a troop of Light Horse, which was active in interdicting Rebel supply lines. Galloway fumed at Howe's failure to fight, writing that "Washington's whole force, being at this time less than 4,000 undisciplined troops, might have been defeated and dispersed, without any difficulty, by a fifth part of the British army."[51]

When spring came, the British unexpectedly abandoned the city, alarmed because the French had entered the war on the side of the Americans. As one British officer who knew him well noted, Galloway was "exposed to the rage of his bitter enemies, deprived of a fortune of about 70,000 pounds, and left to wander like Cain upon the earth without home and without property."[52] He headed the list of traitors promulgated by the new state and his extensive property was forfeited. He fled with the British fleet, leaving his wife behind in a vain attempt to save some of their property. She was evicted from their mansion, her own fortune confiscated, and soon died in poverty.[53]

Galloway went on to England, where he became the *de facto* leader of the large refugee colony, testified before Parliament about England's failure to win the war, and published closely-reasoned, if mooted, treatises on the illegality of the Revolution and the incompetence of the British commanders. When the war ended, Pennsylvania's new government refused to let him return, so he stayed in England, helping his fellow refugees with their claims for compensation from the English government and writing religious treatises.

Galloway was certainly not the only prominent Pennsylvanian to oppose revolution; in fact, most Philadelphians felt the same way. But, since he was the highest-ranking and most articulate Loyalist in the Province and, arguably, in America, his victorious countrymen never forgave him. He backed the wrong side, refused to recant when the tide turned (as did his friend Franklin) and was exiled in disgrace. Had the war gone the other way, he would have been lauded as a hero for following the dictates of his conscience.

At least one other Galloway was an active Loyalist. When Howe occupied Philadelphia, Benjamin Galloway recruited a group of neighbors in Kent County, Delaware, to join the British forces. The rebels retaliated by throwing his wife and children out of his home and into the snow, seizing his cattle, and destroying his farm. He was captured when he came home to rescue his family, but escaped and eventually moved to Canada.[54]

As noted, two of the Baltimore Galloways signed the new government's loyalty oath in 1778, but five refused to do so. Signing was required by law, with stiff penalties for refusing to do so, but Quakers were prohibited from signing by their Meeting. In 1774, when a mob at Annapolis burned a ship to protest the tea tax, John Galloway, (son of Samuel of Tulip Hill) called the event an "infamous and rascally affair which makes all men of property reflect with horror on their present situation to have their lives and propertys at the disposal & mercy of a mob."[55] Despite what we think now, the issues involved in the revolution were far from clear-cut to most Americans of that day.

Chapter 6

Settling Kentucky's Bluegrass

God's and Galloways' Country

If any place deserves to be called "God's country," it is central Kentucky, known as "the Bluegrass" because of the bluish tinge that the rolling grasslands show in spring. Today, those grasslands are set off by plank or stone fences, elegant mansions, and barns that house some of the world's premier racehorses. In the heart of the Bluegrass lies Bourbon County and the pretty town of Paris, with an imposing Palladian courthouse marking its status as the county seat.

Bourbon County is not only God's country, it is Galloway country, for no place is more closely associated with our branch of the family. Galloways have lived there, on and off, for over two hundred years. Some of them, including this writer's parents, paternal grandparents, and various aunts, uncles, and cousins, still rest there, among the fine old trees, winding roads, and centuries-old accumulation of headstones in the Paris City Cemetery.

The town was not chartered until 1786, but Galloways, with other frontiersmen including Simon Kenton and Daniel Boone, were there twenty years earlier. No fort was built at the site, but there was a good spring, so it was often used as an overnight stop for travelers along the Old Buffalo Trace. The town that grew up there was first called Hopewell, a corruption of "hope we'll" (reach the ford tonight), but was changed to Paris in honor of the French, whose intervention had turned the tide in the Revolution. The county, which was formed in 1785, was called Bourbon for the same reason. Bourbon County originally covered so large an area that thirty-three of Kentucky's one hundred counties were later carved out of it.

It used to be said that Kentucky's economy was based on sin: tobacco, whiskey, and horse racing. If you accept the definition, the truism applies precisely to Paris. From the earliest times, whiskey production was a flourishing industry, distilling being an easy way for the pioneers to get their surplus grain to Eastern markets. The county gave its name to Bourbon whiskey, which was first made in Paris, near land then owned by Galloways. Breeding of race horses began as soon as the hostile Indians were cleared out, as did planting of tobacco; both benefited from the fertile soil, with its underlayment of limestone. Hemp, used to make rope, was another important crop.

Kentucky had been "discovered" in 1750, when a party of Virginians found a gap in the wall created by the Allegheny Mountains. The next year, some speculators hired Christopher Gist to explore beyond the mountains. He came down through mountain passes in Western Pennsylvania and made his way through Indian trading villages along the Ohio River to Kentucky. Being warned of hostile tribes in this "dark and bloody ground" (which is a rough translation of the Indian word "Kentucky"), he headed back East. But he had charted a way into the heart of new country that other intrepid souls, including Galloways, would soon follow.

James' Wilderness Travels

James Galloway, (whose Revolutionary Army career we have noted earlier), was one of the "long hunters," Pennsylvania frontiersmen who disappeared beyond the mountains for long periods of time in pursuit of the abundant game there, and who liked the solitary and challenging wilderness life.[56] At the age of 83, James dictated a narrative of his life. Old men forget many things, but not the days of their youth, so his memoir can be taken as an accurate account of the life of a Kentucky pioneer.

The son of George Galloway, James was born and raised on the Pennsylvania frontier. In 1774, at age 24, he and a friend headed out for Kentucky. In his words, "our manner of equipment was a rifle pouch, tomahawk, sun dial, pocket compass, blanket, axe, knapsack and horse." Their food consisted of game that they shot along the way and it is unlikely that they took any change of clothing. Their rifles were too much a part of them to be listed separately as equipment. Following Gist's route, the young men went first to Fort Pitt (the present Pittsburgh), then down the Ohio River in canoes to a point below where Wheeling, West Virginia, now stands, and where there was a small stockade fort. (A map will show how the Ohio snakes down through Pennsylvania into West Virginia, then heads north again to define the line between Kentucky and Ohio; and, while looking at the map, marvel at the distances that James covered on foot, horseback, or by canoe).

The two men hunted in West Virginia for a few months, then left for Kentucky in the company of six Virginians who had been commissioned to build cabins for later settlers. The group went downriver some miles, then struck out by land, "living altogether on meat." At the Upper Blue Licks, north of where Paris now stands, they built eight cabins, for which they drew lots. Then Galloway and his friend "being dissatisfied with the results," (or perhaps tired of the company and the work, or just restless), headed through the woods for Boonesboro, shooting buffalo, deer and bear, "of which there were a great number" along the way.

In the winter of 1775 they arrived at Boonesboro, a rude fort begun in May of that year and consisting of a dozen or so cabins, not yet picketed. This was the first permanent settlement in Kentucky. Richard Henderson of North Carolina and his associates had made a treaty with the Cherokee Indians that granted them all of the land south of the Ohio and north of the Cumberland rivers, (virtually all of Kentucky), and had dispatched Daniel Boone and thirty other men to find a suitable site and to start a settlement.

By the time Galloway arrived, the town had about a dozen

cabins, an unspecified number of men, and six women, the wives
and daughters of Daniel and his brother Squire. The Boones were
also "long hunters" from Pennsylvania and would have welcomed
young Galloway and his rifle, for Indian fighting was fierce. By
1776, there were no more that 200 settlers left in Kentucky, all of
them "forted up" at one of the three settlements there. Galloway
and his friend stayed at the fort for a while and then, along with
the Boone brothers, "engaged to carry chain [survey] for Colonel
Henderson for which they were to receive 1,000 acres." They
quickly tired of that employment and went back to Boonesboro.

James' memoir includes an incident that gives the flavor of his
wanderings. He went from Boonesboro to the lower Blue Licks
and "there for the first time saw Simon Kenton. . . [who] was
then hunting in company with another man and had been there
about six months, and not ever at Boonesborough; came very
near shooting him and had his gun levelled and saw his broad
brimmed hat- holloo'd at him- sat down on the opposite banks
and had a long conversation- at this time was 20 miles from my
comrade. Kenton was making a flint for his gun- was walking
through the country and roving ad libitum."

James and his companion headed back to Pennsylvania on
foot. When they reached the Ohio, the river was so high that their
bark canoes were of no use, so they made rafts on which they laid
"their guns, baggage, etc., which (they swimming) pushed before
them." James was no sooner back in Pennsylvania than he left for
Boston to fight under General Washington and spent the next few
years shooting at Redcoats instead of Indians.

James did not return to Kentucky until 1780, by which time he
had a wife. In company with twenty other families, they built a
fort near Louisville called the Low Dutch Station. He lived there
for about four years, raising corn and supplying the station with
game. (It is not hard to deduce what was James' favorite
occupation). During that time, "scarce a week passed but he was
out after Indians," who "would steal horses and kill men and the
whites would pursue them." The Indians' victims were buried by
putting the dead in holes formed by blowing up trees, then

pulling the dirt-covered roots back down over the bodies and covering them with logs, thus securing the burial and protecting the bodies from mutilation by wild beasts or Indians.

Indian Raids and White Revenge

Indian skirmishes run like a bloody stream through James' narrative, and one marvels not only at his numerous brushes with the Grim Reaper, but at his stamina, courage and luck. Two incidents illustrate his perilous life in Kentucky.

The first story concerns Daniel Boone's brother Squire, who called on the Dutch Station for help when his own fort was attacked. All but seven of the thirty-one men who went to his aid were killed or captured and the militia commander, Colonel Floyd, went out to bury the dead. Galloway promised to join him if he could get a horse, as his had been stolen by Indians.

Just at sundown, Galloway got a mount and started out alone. About a mile from the Station he found himself in the midst of sixteen Indians, led by Simon Girty. Girty, known as the "great renegade," was born in the same part of Pennsylvania as Galloway and Boone, but deserted the American forces during the Revolution to lead British and Indians in raids against them. Fire from two guns, within six inches of Galloway, burned his hands and face, a bullet pierced his arm, and Girty shot him in the shoulder at close range. Bloodied but alive, James escaped and got back to the Station.

The second incident took place a few years later. Some forts near Lexington had been under siege for several days. Finally, one man pulled a board off his house and dropped down outside. He ran to a nearby settlement, which sent out a relief company. This group passed by the fort where James and three of his brothers were living with their families. James wanted to join the rescue party, but they were on horseback and he was again without a mount. By the time he had found one, the men were gone. Galloping to catch up with them, he took a short cut through a cane field, where he was waylaid by twelve Indians. He was not only wounded severely in the left arm, but a ball entered his right side and passed back under his left shoulder.

Inside the fort, James' wife was frantic when she heard the shots and had to be kept from rushing out. But James' luck held. His mount carried him home to the fort, where his nephew happened to look out and saw him lying forward on his horse's neck, covered with blood. James' brother William, who had stayed in the fort to protect the women and children, brought him in, faint from loss of blood.

After a few days, William managed to get to Louisville and bring back a doctor, who dressed James' wounds. Before he left, he gave orders not to remove the dressings. But it was three nights before the doctor could get back; by that time, the left arm had mortified, so the doctor took a razor and cut off the worst part.[57] Let's hope that James, whose skin must have been mostly scar tissue at this point, had a jug of Bourbon County's best-known product handy to help him through his ordeal.

There was no love lost between these men and the Indians. One party of riflemen picked off three braves who were shooting at some whites riding by. They hung one of the dead Indians on a bush by his jaw and carved the flesh from his carcass, then took this back to the fort, where it was roasted and fed to the dogs, "to make them good Indian dogs." (However, William Galloway, who was one of the party, strongly protested this vengeance).

It is easy enough to condemn this barbarism when the only Indians we see are those on a movie or tv screen, but we should remember that the Galloway brothers, who had seen the slaughter at Great Cove, had a different bias. We might also remember that these Indian tribes were apt to mete out equally harsh treatment to their own captives. The commander of a punitive expedition to Pennsylvania's Wyoming Valley in 1779 found the bodies of many settlers, "the savages having put them to the most excrusiating [sic] torments possible by first plucking their nales from hands and feet then spearing, cutting and whipping them and mangling their Bodys, then cuting off the flesh from their shoulders by peices, then Tomahawking and severing their heads from their Bodys and leaving them a prey to their Dogs."[58]

In 1782, James left the Fort for Bourbon County, "where some few deprivations were committed by the Indians." But Indians weren't his only worries. In 1798, he moved north to Ohio, "having been cheated out of his land [in Kentucky]" presumably by later arrivals who may not have been his equal at taming the wilderness, but were better at proving ownership. Early land titles were often disputed, because surveyors lacked proper training or tools, record-keeping was careless, and there were competing claims for the same parcels. Virginia issued warrants for much more land than actually existed, and it was said that enough tracts were claimed for the Bluegrass to cover it four times over.

James' Brothers in Kentucky

James was not the only Galloway to take part in settling Kentucky. His brothers William, John and Samuel came out in 1780 as part of a large company to settle at the Falls of the Ohio, which later became Louisville. Virginia (of which Kentucky was still a part) records of land grants, some of which were given for military service, show that three Galloway brothers were granted land in Kentucky in 1784. John was given 400 acres in Jefferson County (near Louisville), William was given 800 and George 700 acres in Fayette County (near Lexington). Perhaps the Fayette grants were larger because the area was even less settled than Jefferson County.[59] Their father, George, came out to visit, but decided to go on back home to Pennsylvania.

A string of forts a few miles apart were constructed on the trail to Fort Lexington, each consisting of some log houses built around a hollow square, and stockaded on the outside. William lived in these forts for several years, during which time he, John and James left long enough to join General George Rogers Clark's expedition against the Indians at Chillicothe, Ohio.

William then moved on to Lexington, where a few hunters had established themselves in 1775. They had named their settlement after a village in distant Massachusetts, after learning that the first shots of the Revolution had been fired there. William stayed in Lexington several years, going back to Mifflin County, Pennsylvania, long enough to take a wife, who became one of the first four women in Lexington.

Let's pause to pay tribute to these women. William and James and their companions get the glory, but their women had an even harder life. Think of James' wife, wanting to rush out when she heard her husband shot and knowing the Indians were just outside. She probably had at least one child underfoot and another "in the oven." She not only bore and tended the babies, cooked the food, made and mended and washed the clothes, but worked beside her husband in the fields and shared the risks of Indian raids; it was James' grandmother, not his grandfather, who was scalped at Great Cove.

The places where William's children were born mark the route of his travels: the first two in Pennsylvania, the next four in a blockhouse in Lexington, and the last two in Bourbon County. He secured a commissioner's preemption on 1,170 acres of land on the south bank of Stoner Creek and built a cabin where he spent the rest of his days. This is where Paris now stands, although it was then wilderness. The brothers were land-rich but had few worldly possessions. The 1787 census listed James, John and William as living in Bourbon County and owning a total of seven horses and mules, plus 26 head of cattle.

Samuel, the youngest of the four brothers, came out with William to Louisville and later lived a few miles south of Paris. His daughter Ruth married Colonel Richard Henderson, a self-taught lawyer who was Chief Judge of the Province of North Carolina and who had organized the company that hired Daniel Boone to survey Kentucky. Henderson himself later moved to Boonesboro. His wife's sister lived with them and, when Ruth died, she married Henderson, "contrary to the rules of the church," which refused to approve the union.

We will return to Paris and rejoin these Galloways later. But now, we need to go back to Baltimore and pick up other strands of this story.

Chapter 7

Elihu and His Origins

Searching for Thomas

We can trace our Galloway line with absolute certainty back to Thomas Galloway, who died May 18, 1798 in Baltimore County. He left no will, but subsequent court proceedings show that his estate was divided between his wife (whose name we do not know) and five children: Mary (who married Thomas de Moss), Ruth (who married Thomas Farrell), Thomas, William, and Aquilla. Court records make it clear that this William was our ancestor. Thomas' affairs were not settled until 1803, when Ruth sued to force Aquilla to divide the estate: as the only son still alive at that time, he had contested the court valuation of the property. Aquilla then bought out the other heirs and, the next year, sold most of the tract.

Thomas' son (and our ancestor) William had died thirteen years earlier, so his share of his father's estate was divided among his six children, one of whom was still underage in 1803. His will, dated August 10, 1785, stated that he was "weak in body," and left his property to his wife, Mary and his children: Elijah, Elizabeth, Sarah, Jemina, Elisha, and Elihu. The Biblical names Elijah, Elisha and Elihu may have resulted from the "Great Awakening," a religious revival that swept the country in the early 1740's. In the Bible's Book of Kings, Elijah went to Heaven in a Chariot of Fire, and Elisha inherited his spirit. Ejihu, although young, taught wisdom to Job in the Book of that name.

Another child was born after his death, but died at birth. William died some time before October 24, when his will was probated. His brother, Thomas Jr., did not long outlive their father, for he died in 1802. In 1781, he had married Catherine Dallas and their five children (Walter, Parmelia, William, Thomas, and John) were all under 21 years of age at the time of his death.

We do not know the name of Thomas Sr.'s father; he is the "missing link" that ties our proven ancestry to earlier generations. There are, however, several candidates for the position. To sort these out, we have four kinds of clues: (1) locations; (2) dates; (3) names; and (4) religious affiliations.

(1) Locations. We know exactly where William and his father were living at the time of their deaths, for both had property in My Lady's Manor, a tract of land which was located in Baltimore County at present-day Monkton. The Manor was on the Gunpowder River, which bordered the Harford County line, and about twenty miles from the Pennsylvania state line. It consisted of 10,000 acres belonging the Proprietor of Maryland, Lord Baltimore, which had been confiscated during the Revolution, then divided into lots and sold by the government, often to people who were already leasing the same lot.

Court records concerning their estates show that Thomas first leased and then purchased 171.25 acres in the Manor, consisting of part of lot 12 and all of lot 13. William had purchased lot 14, consisting of 122 acres, part of which were in Harford County. He had not had a chance to occupy the lot by the time of his death in 1785, but the court granted title to his widow. Land in the Manor was also leased to her father, Daniel Pocock.[60]

As noted earlier, Maryland land was divided into areas called "hundreds." My Lady's Manor was in Mine Run Hundred, which was created in 1758 out of Gunpowder Upper Hundred. In 1692, when the Assembly made the Anglican Church the state religion, Maryland was officially divided into parishes, which were required to register all births, marriages, and deaths. My Lady's Manor was in St. James Parish, which was created in 1750 out of St. John's Parish; while this parish's records are incomplete, they show that not only William, but his brother and sister were

married there.

(2) Dates. William was probably still quite young when he died in 1785, for he had been married in 1774 and one of his children had still not come of age by 1803. By that time, William's brother had also died, leaving five minor children, which indicates that he, too, was fairly young. If we speculate that William was at least 18 years old when he married in 1774, and that his father was at least 18 when he was born, Thomas (who died in 1798) must have been born no later than 1738, and probably some years earlier.

(3) Names. First-born sons were usually named after their paternal grandfathers. Thomas named his eldest son after himself, but his second son was named William and the third Aquilla, so there is a good chance that was his father's name was William, and that he had a relative named Aquilla.

The name Aquila (which is the Latin word for Eagle and was sometimes spelled Acquila or Aquilla), was unusual even at that time, but was found among the West River Galloways. In 1722, Joseph Galloway of West River married the daughter of Aquilla Paca and, in 1731, his brother Richard married her sister. In 1743, wills were recorded for Aquila Galloway and Aquila Paca at West River.

(4) Religion. The Anne Arundel County Galloways were Quakers, as were at least some Baltimore County Galloways. Records of the Bush River Meeting House for 1728 refer to a John, Joseph, Moses and Richard Galloway. In 1778, Thomas Galloway Sr. signed a loyalty oath to the new government, but Thomas Jr., John, and Moses refused to do. Quakers were forbidden by the Meeting to sign the oath, although refusal carried heavy penalties. As Quakers could not bear arms, it is also worth noting that neither William nor his brothers served in the Continental forces, although they were of an age to do so.

Using these four guidelines, we can try and identify William's father Thomas. The name appears in several reliable records; looking at some of these in chronological order, we find that:

-in 1704, Thomas Galloway recorded a cattle mark, "a Cropp

and two Slitts in each Ear," in Anne Arundel County, and in 1717 he witnessed a land sale there. These are the only references to a Thomas Galloway in Maryland until the name appears in Baltimore County in 1768. While the Anne Arundel County Thomas is clearly not William's father (who died in 1798), he might be his grandfather, and might have been kin to the William who left there in the late 1600's and founded the Cecil/Baltimore county line of Galloways.

-a 1783 tax list for Mine Run Hundred shows that Thomas and William were at My Lady's Manor by that date. It also notes that Thomas' household had three males and two females, as well as seven horses and eight cattle, while William's had two males and one female, as well as five horses and four cattle. We know that this Thomas and William are our ancestors, because the acreages shown on the tax lists match those shown in the settlement of their estates. The list for Gunpowder Upper Hundred, which joins Mine Run, shows an Aquila, presumably William's brother, with fifty acres and a household of eight persons, including five males. The third brother, Thomas Jr., was listed at Back River Hundred, which adjoins Mine Run, with 78 acres, two males and one female.

-In 1790, the first federal census lists a Thomas as head of household in Mine Run Hundred, along with one other adult male, one male under 16 years of age, and two females. The other male was probably his son Aquila, since the other two sons had married and presumably moved out by that date.

A Persuasive Possibility

Available records simply do not give any clear answers about Thomas' ancestry. But these records are full of errors, contradictions, and omissions, which may explain the absence of a clear path to Thomas.

The most persuasive possibility is that Thomas was the son of William Galloway, who died in Baltimore County in 1743, and who was descended from the William who bought land there in

1667; his ancestry has been traced in the discussion of the Baltimore Galloways. (To lessen confusion, we shall call him William III, since his father and grandfather were also named William). William III died in 1743. His will left his estate to his widow, Priscilla Carr, and seven children, who were named in the will as Moses, William (who we shall call William IV), Selathial, Absalom, Aquila, Elizabeth and Mephitica. Parish and other official records show that he was married on August 9, 1725, and give the birth dates of some, but not all, of these children, although some dates are inconsistent. The eldest child, Moses, was born in 1726, so all of William III's children would have been under age at the time of his death.

Under the will, the widow was left one-third of the land, Moses inherited a 47 acre tract called "Mary's Adventure" plus 87 acres of a 486 tract called "Galloway's Enlargement," while William got 132 acres of the latter and "the dwelling plantation," which was probably a 48 acre tract called "White Oak Thicket." Subtracting the widow's third and these two sons shares from the deceased's total land holdings, only 107 acres were left for the other three sons.

A strong argument can be made that our Thomas was another of William III's sons, perhaps by a previous marriage, in which case he probably would have come of age by the time William III died. He might have been disinherited because of a family quarrel, or because he was sufficiently established that he did not need his portion of an estate that was already stretched too thin; if he were not to inherit, he would not have been named in the will.

Another possibility is that there could have been a confusion over names (as was often the case), and the son listed as William IV could actually have been our Thomas. Records were inexact; William IV's brother Salethial is listed elsewhere as Jalathiel, and his sister Mephitica as Mophitica. There is definitely confusion as to this William's birthdate, which is shown in various records as ranging from September 2, 1726, to February 2, 1729, while there is agreement on the birthdates of his siblings. While the other sons' marriages are documented, William IV's is not.

The name William appears on various tax and other lists of Gunpowder and Middle River hundreds, but we can't be certain whether this is our ancestor Thomas' son, or someone else. In 1774, a son named Thomas was born to "William of Timonium." Timonium was the home of Thomas III and his son; however, our ancestor William was in the same area and was married early in 1774, so the baby Thomas might have been a son of his, who died too soon to be named in his father's will. Another possibility is that the child was actually Thomas, Jr., and that the father's name was given incorrectly.

Adding to the confusion is a William who died in 1801 "at his seat in Middle River Neck," which is south of the Gunpowder River. He married Anne Waller in 1792 and had a son named William and a daughter named Priscilla, which was the name of William III's wife. He served in the Militia in 1776 and 1777, but refused to sign the 1778 loyalty oath. However, militia records give his birth date as November 21, 1738, which is too far from the dates usually given for William IV (February 2, 1728 or 1729) to be explained by the frequent carelessness about such matters.

While nothing can be proved conclusively, we can use the four sets of clues offered earlier to come up with persuasive evidence in support of our theory that our Thomas was the son of William III.

(1) Locations. William III was a "Gunpowder River" Galloway. His marriage, the births of most of his children, and these children's' marriages are recorded in St. Johns (later St. James) Parish, as are the marriages of Thomas' children. Property records show that this parish was where William and Thomas, as well as their children, were situated.

(2) Dates. We have postulated that Thomas was born no later than 1738, and probably much earlier. Existing records give the birth dates of William III's eldest sons as follows: Moses, September 2, 1726; William, September 2, 1726, or January 2, 1728 or 1729; Salathiel, December 3, 1730. Not only is there confusion as to the year of William's birth (leaving the possibility

that there may have been more than one birth recorded), but there is adequate time between these three children to allow for another birth.

(3) Names. Thomas named his eldest son after himself, but his next was named William, and a son was customarily given the name of his paternal grandfather. His third son had the unusual name of Aquila, which was the name of one of William III's sons. Another of William III's sons had the unusual name of Salathiel; at the time of Thomas' death in 1798, a Salathiel Galloway (who was almost certainly the same man) was living in a cabin owned by Thomas on the Gunpowder River. This Salathiel had married (to Mary Galloway) the year before, so was probably too young to be William III's son, but the name makes it all but certain that he was a relative. (Thomas, Jr., named his sons Thomas, William and Jehu; Thomas, Jr., in turn, gave the name to one of his sons, and named another Moses, perhaps after William III's eldest son).[61]-

Thomas' name appears along with William III's sons Moses and Aquilla on a 1768 petition to move the county seat to Baltimore; this was also signed by William, who may have been their brother or, more probably, Thomas' son. Aquila and William are on a 1773 list of taxables in Middle River and Gunpowder hundreds, but Thomas is not, indicating that he did not own land there at that time. A 1778 list of those who signed or refused to sign a loyalty oath includes Thomas and Thomas, Jr., along with John and Moses.

The 1790 federal census for Mine Run Hundred lists William's widow Mary, Thomas Sr. and Thomas Jr. as heads of household. Mary's household had four females, two boys under 16, and one slave. One Thomas' household included two adult males, one boy and two females, and the other had one man, four boys, and two females; neither had slaves. Also listed in Baltimore Count were Aquila, John, James, Moses, and William. John and James are Moses sons; Aquila may have been his brother, but was probably Thomas' son. Moses, incidentally, was quite wealthy, and owned 23 slaves.

(4) Religion. As we have seen, Thomas, Jr. (our Thomas' son) refused to sign a loyalty oath in 1778, as did Moses and his son John, which indicates that both families had at least some members who were Quakers. The only Baltimore County Galloway to take up arms was the William Galloway mentioned above, which is another indication that they may have been Quakers.

The final, and perhaps strongest, argument for naming the William who died in 1743 as our missing ancestor is a negative one: there are simply no other candidates who meet the criteria for Thomas' father. William of Dorchester County, who died in 1750, was not only in the wrong location, but was probably too old as his wife was only 37 when he died. The just-mentioned Patriot William was in the area, but was too young. There are no records of Thomas' birth and he is not named in any wills.

Our Ancestor William

We can't prove Thomas' ancestry, but his descendants' names and dates are well documented. The Records of St. John's Parish in Harford County show that his son William was married on February 20, 1774 to Mary Pocock, who was then 17 years old and was one of Daniel and Sarah Eleanor Jones Pocock's twelve children. Her grandfather, also named Daniel Pocock, was in Maryland by 1730, when he bound one of his sons as an apprentice, and a Daniel Pocock, probably her father, was living at Forks of Gunpowder in 1752.

In 1792, William's brother Acquila married Ann Barton and, in 1794, his sister Ruth married Thomas Farrell. His sister Mary married John De Moss, but we do not know when. There are puzzling gaps of eighteen and twenty years, a whole generation, between the dates of William's marriage and those of his two siblings. There is also a gap in the ages of their families, as all but one of William's children came of age while Thomas' were still minors. A probable explanation is that Thomas, Sr., was married twice and William was the child of his first wife, with some years elapsing before he remarried and fathered the other children. Unfortunately, his will does not give his wife's name.

William's will, made two months before his death, left one-third of his estate "and also a mare and a bed" to his "beloved wife," who was sole executor. The rest of his property went to six children, who were, in order of birth, Elijah, Elizabeth, Sarah, Jemina, Elisha, and Elihu. The eldest son was named after his wife's younger brother and the second daughter after her mother. We do not know why he chose the other names, but it is probable that his mother was named Elizabeth. Elisha may have been named after a neighbor; a 1798 tax list for Mine Run Hundred lists an Elisha Gorsuch, and William's daughter Sarah married a John Gorsuch, probably Elisha's son, in 1795; they were presumably descendants of the Robert Gorsuch whose cabin on the Gunpowder River was plundered by Indians in 1661.

Elihu's mother, Mary Pocock Galloway, was left a widow with six children and another (who would die at birth) on the way. She was not well provided for; in addition to the land, William's worldly goods included a mare, eleven sheep, ten cows, and one Negro man named James. When his affairs were settled, each child's share of their father's estate was only 18 pounds, 13 shillings. In 1803, each also inherited 23 pounds, 17 shillings from their grandfather Thomas.

Elihu's Kentucky Connections

We may not know much about William, but military pension, census, and other reliable records track his son Elihu's life. Elihu (sometimes spelled Elihue) was a roamer. He was born in Maryland in 1784, moved to Kentucky prior to 1807, and died in Indiana in 1863.[62]

In 1794, nine years after her first husband's death, Elihu's mother married Francis Hare in Baltimore. Soon after, her twenty-year old son Elijah moved to Bourbon County, Kentucky, taking along ten-year old Elihu. The 1790 Maryland census lists Mary as head of household with two boys under 16 years of age, three other females, and one slave. Elijah and Elihu were close, for Elihu later named a son after Elijah. Perhaps they left home because they didn't get along with their stepfather, or perhaps Elijah wanted to strike out on his own and join relatives on the Kentucky frontier. His mother, Mary Pocock Galloway, would have understood this urge to move on, for three of her siblings, including Elijah, had already moved to Ohio.

The first Kentucky reference to Elihu was in 1807, when he would have been 23 years old. His name appears on a delinquent tax list for Fleming County,[63] showing that he owned land there at the time, although he did not necessarily live on it. Fleming County was named after two brothers who built a fort there in 1787, after coming down the Ohio River; this is the route taken by the Pennsylvania Galloways who came to Kentucky in 1774, and probably followed by Elihu. In 1800, Elijah had married Nancy West in Mason County, Kentucky; Nancy's family apparently was from Harford County, Maryland, so he had probably known her there.

In March of 1811, Elihu married Mary "Polly" Elliott, daughter of William and Martha Elliott. They were married by a Presbyterian minister in the thriving town of Paris, which was described a few years earlier as having "a handsome situation" and consisting of about one hundred houses and stores, with two streets running through.[64] Elihu's brother Elijah and his sister Elizabeth moved to Paris at some point, for their deaths were later recorded there. Another sister, Jemima, married a Baltimore neighbor, Jesse Hutchins, and moved to Ohio, where the couple spent the rest of their lives. So at least three of William Galloway's children went to Kentucky and one went north to Ohio.

Elihu's mother and step-father did not make the move, for the 1810 census shows Frank Hare still in Baltimore County, In 1799, Elijah deeded his share of his father's Maryland land to his sister Sarah. In 1800, she and another sister, Jemima deeded their shares to their step-father, as did Elihu when he received his inheritance in 1806, after coming of age. The records do not show whether Hare paid his step-children for the land.[65]

It seems safe to say that these Galloways moved to Kentucky to join relatives who were already there. In 1794, when Elihu's mother remarried, the four Galloway brothers who had explored Kentucky were all in or around Paris: William would die there in 1795, and John would act as his executor; James moved to Ohio, but not until 1798; and Samuel apparently lived there until his death.

These pioneer brothers sired another generation of Galloways, some of whom would have been Elihu's contemporaries. When William died in 1794, he left a wife, Rebekah, and seven children: William, John, James, Joseph, Mary, Ann, and Rebekah. James' children, some of who went to Ohio with him, but some of who may have stayed in Kentucky, were named James, Joseph, William, Samuel, Rebecca, Andrew, and Anthony. We don't know what names John and Samuel gave to their children, but they probably included the usual ones.

William's family came on hard times after his death. His wife Rebeckah, who had shared much of his life on the frontier, remarried; it was hard for a widow to manage on her own. But she chose badly, for her new husband, Ezekial Mitchell, turned out to be a drunkard. In 1803, a suit was brought claiming that he "has wantonly committed waste" on land she held for her children "by cutting great quantities of timber." Another suit enjoined him from selling land assigned as her dower and leaving her without support. She charged that, although she had "lived with him since marriage and conducted herself in a decent and discreet manner, shortly after marriage she found he has given himself wholly to intoxication and seemed to be wasting what property she possessed, refused her to keep her children, had them sent away and brought two of his own children for [her] to care for." Despite this, "she would have continued living with him had not she been in danger of losing her life."[66]

Elihu gave some of his sons the names of the Kentucky Galloways, adding support to the theory that they were related. These boys, in order of age, were named William, Samuel, John,

Robert, Joseph, Elisha, Ephriam, and George Washington. His father had been named William (and so was his father-in-law, with whom he later moved to Indiana) and his oldest brother was named Elijah, but the other names are not found in his own or his father's family. Samuel, Joseph and John may named after Kentucky kinfolk, and the youngest boy's name is a nod to Elihu's patriotism.

It would be reasonable to assume that Elihu and his brother had gone to Paris to join kinfolk who were already living there, and whose history we have already described. A 1790 tax list shows John, James, and William Galloway owning land in Bourbon County (James' father had left him his "best hat" along with land warrants for 500 acres), and a census for the same year showed William, James and John in Baltimore County.

By 1800, only two Galloways, Catherine and Ezekiel, were left in Baltimore County. The family, like so many other settlers, had moved west with the frontier.

Chapter 8

Two Wars and a Troubled Peace

Patriots in the War of 1812

Thirty years after the Treaty of Paris had ratified America's independence, the new Nation's survival remained tenuous. Britain was focused on the Napoleonic wars in Europe, but her ships still roamed America's shores and would sometimes impress her sailors and blockade her ports. The British still held Canada and backed the Shawnee Chief Tecumseh's efforts to organize a tribal coalition to halt Americans' westward expansion.

In June of 1812, after sporadic clashes, President Madison asked Congress to declare war with Britain. The war was triggered mainly by maritime disputes, but was fought largely along the frontier, which then ran through Ohio, Michigan and Indiana. The frontier supplied not only the battle sites, but most of the men who fought the battles, including some Galloways ancestors.

Kentucky had a special stake in the war. The state had sent volunteer troops to augment William Henry Harrison's regular forces at the battle of Tippecanoe, and many had been killed by Tecumseh's braves. As James' adventures show, the state had been wrested from the Indians by the rifle, and its citizens had no love for the Indians, nor for the British who were arming them. Kentucky's own Henry Clay led the "warhawk" faction in Congress and pro-war rallies were held throughout the state.

Kentuckians greeted the news that war had been declared with celebrations, and Richard Matson's company, a unit made up mostly of Bourbon County volunteers, soon marched north to meet the enemy. On January 18, 1813, after five months in the field, Matson's unit was part of the force sent to save Frenchtown, on the frozen shores of Lake Erie, from approaching British troops and Indian braves. The freezing, starving Americans were nearing the Raisin River when they met the British. After being exhorted by their commander to remember that "You have the double character of Americans and Kentuckians to sustain," they attacked, won the battle, and occupied Frenchtown.

The British brought in troops from nearby garrisons, then joined with the Indians in attacking Frenchtown on the 22nd, defeating the outnumbered and exhausted Americans. A few escaped, but most, including about 65 wounded, were left in the town. The next day, while the British stood by and watched, the Indians massacred the wounded, mutilated their corpses, and burned the town. The surviving prisoners were taken to a British fort, where the Indians decorated the stockades with heads of fallen Americans. When news of the atrocity reached Kentucky, an angry legislature authorized additional militia units , which the Governor himself then led north to battle.

In August of 1813, the 28-year-old Elihu Galloway said goodbye to his bride of a year, grabbed his flintlock, and joined Matson's militia as a cavalry private.[67] He had to supply his own clothing and equipment. If he followed the prevailing fashion, this consisted of:

> . . . a hunting shirt made of linsey. . . his pants were of Kentucky jeans and he walked in shoes or moccasins, as was his fancy. . . Across his shoulder was the strap that held up his powder horn, in which strap was another leather case containing his formidable butcher knife and another to hold his bullets. A knapsack of home manufacture contained his clothing, and the outside of it was garnished with a glittering tin cup.[68]

Elihu fought in the Battle of the Thames, which took place in Ontario on October 5, 1813, under General William Henry

Harrison. (A Samuel Galloway, from Scott County, Kentucky, who was probably a relative, was in the same battle). After the order to charge went through the ranks, a cry rose from the nearly six hundred Kentuckians along the line: "Remember the Raisin." Driven by the memory of their murdered countrymen, the men soundly defeated the British and their Indian allies, thereby restoring American dominance in the Northwest.

One far-reaching result of the battle was the death of the great Shawnee Chief Tecumseh; the British General fled the field, but the Indian leader stood, fought, and died there. Without his leadership, the confederacy he had built began to disintegrate and his braves deserted the British cause.

Tecumseh had been a frequent visitor at the home of James Galloway in Chillicothe, Ohio, where James had moved in 1795. The Chief became close friends with James' daughter, Rebekah, who taught him the Bible, Shakespeare and history, and told him of Alexander, Caesar, and other heroes of the past. Their friendship ripened into a romance. In 1807, when Rebekah turned 16, Tecumseh gave her a birchbark canoe and asked for her hand in marriage, giving her a month to decide. When the time was up, Tecumseh took her out on the Scioto River in the canoe to hear her answer. She reluctantly told him that she would marry him only if he would take up the White man's way of life. Torn between his love for her and the claims of his own heritage, the Chief could not bring himself to abandon his people, so his visits to Rebekah grew fewer and his efforts to organize the Indian confederacy intensified, ultimately leading to war.

True to Galloway tradition, Rebekah later married a cousin, George Galloway. In 1926, their grandson, William Galloway, (who was both a physician and a lawyer), of Xenia, Ohio, visited Tecumseh's great-grandson on an Oklahoma reservation, and the two men joined in smoking a "peace pipe" that the great Chief had given James Galloway in 1797.

Other Galloway men who served in the War of 1812 included Daniel in the Kentucky militia, John (or Jehu) in Wilson's Virginia Militia, (although he was married and died in

Baltimore), John (from Mifflin County) in the Pennsylvania Militia, and Samuel in the Ohio Rangers.

Elihu Moves North

When the war ended, Congress granted land in the newly-secured territories of Ohio and Indiana to those veterans who would agree to settle there. Elihu Galloway was awarded 120 acres in Indiana and moved north with his family in 1817 to occupy them. He and his wife Polly had eleven children: William, Sara, Elihu, Samuel, John, Martha, Robert, Joseph, Elisha, Ephriham, and George Washington, the eldest born in 1811 and the youngest in 1834. Samuel, who was this writer's great-grandfather, was born in Kentucky, before his father moved north.[69]

Another veteran who took up bounty land was Robert Bryerly (spelled Brierly in some records), who was given 160 acres for his service in the 17th Infantry. He had enlisted in May, 1814, giving his occupation as a blacksmith, and served until June, 1815. There was some confusion about his eligibility, as, even by the war's end, he was not old enough to be a soldier. A closer look at the records revealed that he had enlisted as a drummer boy at the tender age of 14. He served in the same unit as his father, who was also named Robert, and who also received a land grant. The boy-soldier is part of our ancestry for, in 1832, young Bryerly married Jane Simonin, of whose family we shall hear more later; in 1886, their granddaughter would marry Elihu Galloway's grandson.

Elihu went to Indiana with his father-in-law, William Elliot, who was one of the original purchasers in Jennings County, buying land there in 1818. Elliot was also a veteran, having been an officer in the Revolutionary War. He came from Pennsylvania to Bourbon County, where records show he was living as early as 1787, when he was evicted from his homestead after a title dispute.

His plight was not uncommon. Kentucky had never been

surveyed by the federal government, so settlers defined the land they claimed by reference to landmarks such as waterways or even specific trees. The result was a morass of conflicting claims which had to be settled through litigation. Small farmers seldom could afford attorneys' fees to defend their claims, so often lost their land, and the work that had gone into clearing it.

Arriving at his farm in Indiana, the 31-year-old Elihu built a log cabin up on a high cliff (and one hopes that he was able to expand it as babies kept arriving). A descendant who recently visited the farm called the area "Godforsaken," but it probably was more promising when Elihu lived there, before the thin soil had been farmed out. This was hilly country, in contrast to the rich soil of Bourbon County. Elihu remained there until his death in 1863, at the age of 78, and rests with his wife, (who lived to the age of 87), in the cemetery at Zenas, Indiana, about 50 miles northeast of Louisville.

Other Galloways were among the original landholders in Jennings County. William, Samuel and Elijah Galloway bought land there at various dates from 1837 to 1839; they were presumably Elihu's sons, all of whom would have been in their twenties. Elisha Galloway, probably Elihu's older brother, bought land in 1817.[70] Indiana was a tamer frontier than Galloways had known in Pennsylvania and Kentucky; gone were the days of the long hunters, abundant game, solitary wanderings in the forests, and bloody encounters with Indians, a world erased by a wave of settlers.

Back to Kentucky

Much of this story has shown our ancestors as fighting men, skirmishing with Indians or battling the British in two wars. But the mid-Nineteenth Century was a time of peace. The Compromise of 1850 held the Union together by maintaining a precarious balance between free and slave states, but another decade would unleash a devastating civil war.

As the 1850's began, our ancestor Samuel Galloway (Elihu's

son, born May 20, 1816), was farming in Bracken County, in northern Kentucky. By 1851, Samuel had three sons; seven more children would be born before his family was complete. His offspring kept arriving with great regularity, the first in 1842 and the last in 1866.

At the age of 28, Samuel had married 16-year-old Elizabeth "Betsey" Wyatt, (1828-1889), the fifth of Henry and Elizabeth Wyatt's eleven children. These Wyatts were Virginians who moved to Pendleton County, Kentucky, in the early 1780's, soon after their marriage.[71] Henry had served as a private in the 7th Virginia Regiment during the Revolutionary War and had fought in the battle of Monmouth. He was of distinguished lineage, being descended from Reverend Haute Wyatt, who had come to Virginia with his brother Sir Francis Wyatt, the first Governor of the Colony, and who had served as Rector at Jamestown from 1621-1625.

Samuel Galloway had grown up in Indiana, but returned to Kentucky in 1840, when Bracken County records show a note he gave for buying some farm implements. The note was paid off two years later, with his Uncle Elijah signing as a witness. He bought a 276 acre farm bordering Willow Creek. In his later years, he ran the Phoenix Hotel in Falmouth, which he had taken as payment for a debt, perhaps preferring the conviviality of innkeeping to the isolation of farm life.

Samuel and Betsy are buried in the churchyard at Willow, in Bracken County. When he died in 1896, the list of items auctioned to settle his modest estate included not only thirty-nine sheep and thirty-two lambs and an assortment of farm implements and household items, but fourteen books, plus the Bible. The books, which were bought by relatives, fetched from one to fifty-three cents each, while the livestock brought a total of $106.

According to one source, two of Samuel's brothers (John and George) stayed in Indiana, two (Elijah and William) went west to Missouri, and one (Robert) moved to Iowa.[72] The Indians had been driven out of the midwest, the War of 1812 had brought an end to foreign efforts to claim American territory, and there was nothing to stem the flow of people westward. From sea to shining sea, it was all one nation, and the Galloways, like other families, were free to spread out.

The Galloways' motives for moving were varied. A grandson of Samuel recalled that one of his uncles went west just ahead of the sheriff, after burning down another farmer's barn during the "tobacco wars," when Kentucky farmers banded together and cut production to force the tobacco companies to pay decent prices for their crops. Harsh reprisals were taken against neighbors who didn't cooperate; after two centuries, the golden leaf was still the mid-South's cash crop.

The Civil War

In the Presidential election of 1860, Kentucky had voted against its two native sons, Abraham Lincoln and John C. Breckinridge, in favor of John Bell of Tennessee, who promised to save the Union at any cost. (Breckinridge would go on to be a Major General in the Confederate Army and command a division at Stone's River, while his brother became a General in the Union army; one of their progenitors had been a witness to William Galloway's will in 1795, and one of their descendants, another John Breckinridge, would become Attorney General of Kentucky and a close friend of this writer).

Kentucky was a slave state, but many of its people favored keeping the Union intact, so it remained neutral in the war. But, true to its bloody beginnings, the state lost more men proportionately than any other state, although they fought on both sides, while bands of soldiers in both Blue and Grey roamed and often skirmished within its borders..

In 1862, Samuel Galloway, who was now a farmer in Pendleton County, Kentucky, near the Ohio River, heard of the victories that General Grant was winning, the first good news for the Union in this War that seemed to be going all wrong. Samuel's people came from a line of fighters, but he was 46 years old, with eight children and another on the way. The oldest boys were aged 16 and 14, not old enough to enlist or to manage the farm if he left to join up. So Samuel spent the war farming his land and taking care of his family.

Part of his land was wooded, so he managed to hide his livestock when troops came through, as they sometimes did. His grandson, Floyd Emerson Galloway, remembered hearing that Samuel started out with some southern sympathies, as he owned a few slaves, but became strongly pro-Union after Confederate raiders swept through the area, foraging as they went.

Samuel was clearly a patriot; his first son was named Elihu, after his father, but his second son was named after William Henry Harrison, the hero of the War of 1812, who became President in 1840. Another of his ten children was named George Washington. The third son was John Robert, but the fourth, who was born on March 4, 1863, was named Ulysses Simpson Grant, after the General who had just given the battered Union a much-needed victory by taking Fort Donelson and would henceforth be known as "Unconditional Surrender" Grant for the terms he demanded.

At least one Galloway who was probably kin to our line did fight for the Union. Joseph D. Galloway was with a Pennsylvania regiment and kept a diary that is still extant; his name and state make it likely that he was a relative.[73] So far as we know, none of our ancestors fought for the Confederacy.

Chapter 9

The French Connection

Fleeing the Guillotine

This chapter is clearly a digression from the Galloway's history, but is included because it is a fascinating, if forgotten, example of the melting pot that is America.

Our Galloway forbearers and the families they married into are solidly British, with one exception: the great-grandparents of Grant Galloway's wife, Alice Moreland, were French.[74]

During the reign of terror that followed the French Revolution, the Scioto Company opened an office in Paris to sell lands on the Ohio River. The company alleged that it owned three million acres, bought from the Ohio Company, a group of Bostonian speculators who had purchased the land from the government at the bargain price of a dollar per acre. A prospectus offered to the Parisians described a rich land with fine mill sites, abundant water power, large deposits of coal and iron, and silver and gold mines in a land inhabited by friendly natives who were eager to provide the necessary labor to reap these riches in return for a few bright beads.

The promoters' glowing descriptions of this Arcadian spot quickly attracted nervous aristocrats and the artisans who served them, all of whom were undoubtedly heartbroken to leave their beloved country, but were anxious to get out from the shadow of *La Guillotine* while they still had their heads intact. About five hundred of them (or six hundred by some accounts) sailed from the port of Havre de Grace and headed for America. They sailed in half a dozen vessels, the largest number embarking in February of 1790. Due to adverse winds and scanty nautical skills, most of their ships did not reach Virginia until the following May, by which time the passengers must have wished they'd never left the cobbled, albeit blood-soaked, streets of Paris.

Once ashore in Virginia, their troubles continued. While they were cordially welcomed by Americans, who were still grateful for French aid that had been crucial to defeating the British in the Revolutionary War, the new arrivals learned to their dismay that they had been duped by persuasive but dishonest salesmen . The lands they had bought were not in a settled and cultivated area, as they had been promised, but were far to the west, in a raw wilderness inhabited only by hostile savages.

Matters worsened when the titles to the land for which they'd paid good gold turned out to be worthless; the land actually still belonged to The Ohio Company, the Scioto Company having failed to pay for its purchase. Efforts to make the latter company reimburse the emigrants failed, and many of the Frenchmen abandoned their claims and went instead to New York and Philadelphia. But some remained in Virginia, persisting in their plan to found a new settlement in the west.

Finally, President Washington intervened and persuaded the Scioto Company not only to transport the stranded French immigrants up the Ohio River, but to send a crew to survey and to lay out a town, to be divided among them according to how much they had paid in Paris, and to build blockhouses for defense against Indian attacks.

In June of 1790, the work party arrived at the site of what was to be Gallipolis, after the ancient name of the settlers' homeland, and began building forts and cabins. Most of the colonists arrived in October, after an arduous journey by wagons and boats. But all was not well, for:

> Imagine five hundred emigrants from the thickly-populated
> districts of France, composed entirely of those who were in
> perfect ignorance of what would be required of them in a new

country- physicians, lawyers, jewelers and other artisans, a few mechanics, servants to the exiled nobility, and many with no trade or profession- suddenly placed in a wilderness of this kind, infested by ferocious wild beasts, and still more murderous bands of lawless Indians.

The settlers, most of whom were aristocrats, their servants, and the skilled and specialized tradesmen who supplied them with luxury goods, did not include any hunters, soldiers, carpenters, woodsmen or practitioners of other ordinary trades that were essential to survive in this untamed wilderness. Later, those settlers who made it through the early months would hire men with less refined backgrounds to do this work for them, but, without these skills, many of them died during the particularly harsh winter that followed. They were threatened with starvation, for the supplies they had brought with them were exhausted, the Scioto Company stopped furnishing provisions, and the Ohio was frozen over so nothing could be brought in by boat.

These babes in the woods did have one bit of luck, though, without which the little settlement probably would have perished entirely: the Indians in the area mistakenly assumed that the newcomers were from the French settlements in Canada, with which they had friendly relations, so left the defenseless newcomers unmolested.

Even with the Indian threat neutralized, only half of the original five hundred or so emigrants survived their first four years in Gallipolis, and it was not until 1796 that an Act of Congress granted them valid title to their lands. Two of those hardy survivors, Lewis Peter LeClere and his wife Louisa Constance, whose surname we do not know, were great-great grandparents of Alice Josephine Moreland, who would marry Samuel Galloway's son Grant. The LeClere's daughter Athalic married a fellow-Frenchman, Francis Simonin, and his daughter, Jane Simonin, married Robert Brierly, whose daughter Eliza Ann was Alice Moreland's mother. Alice Moreland Galloway apparently kept in touch with her French forebearers for, in 1890, she left her Kentucky home to visit her grandmother Jane Simonin in Gallipolis.

We do not know what was the economic status of these particular members of the French settlement, or from what part of France they came. But we do know that they, like the early Galloway settlers, obviously had courage, perseverance, and that equally essential quality for pioneers, a lot of luck.

Chapter 10

Some Kentucky Descendants

As the 19th Century came to a close, so did America's frontier. Out West, the surviving Indians had been driven onto reservations, where they and their descendants would be left to subsist at a near-starvation level, without purpose or hope. The massive herds of buffalo had been slaughtered and the Great Plains turned to farmland. In the East, an influx of immigrants and the growing strength of organized labor fed unrest in the cities. Congress grappled with legislation to curb the giant trusts that were strangling the economy while making fortunes for their organizers.

In Kentucky, Cassius Marcellus Clay, Jr. presided over a state constitutional convention. In his acceptance speech, Clay talked of the "wonderful changes" that had taken place in the state, noting that "every conceivable implement of machinery to aid production, transportation and manufacture has been invented," and "the brain of our people, stimulated by training and education, has in every department achieved the grandest triumphs."[75] But Kentucky, like other states, was in the throes of a depression brought on in large part by monetary policies and by the trusts' control of everything from the price of farm products to the costs of shipping. Times were hard on the farm; but then, they almost always were.

The Morelands

On February 28, 1886, in Pendleton County, Kentucky, Samuel's son Ulysses Simpson Grant Galloway (who used the name Grant) married Alice Josephine Moreland. We will now digress to look at the bride's family.

Alice Moreland's great-grandfather Samuel Moreland was born in Charles County, Maryland in 1764, the son of Richard Moreland and Elizabeth Cooksey Moreland. His grandfather Philip's will had been recorded in Charles County in 1766, so the family must have come to America prior to that date.[76] By 1811, when Elihu Galloway married Polly Elliott in Bourbon County, Kentucky, Samuel Moreland was living in the adjoining county, Bath, with his wife Elancer Shields and his three-year-old son John.

Alice's father, David, operated a carding factory, but his success was undermined by a weakness for drink. His father, John, was a photographer who also served as a Methodist circuit rider. There were not enough ministers to serve the scattered settlements, so the Methodists (an English sect that came to America about the time of the Revolution), had a system whereby a minister, instead of serving a single church, rode a "circuit" to visit remote farms, where he would hold services and perform baptisms and marriages in a cabin or out in the open. The devotion of these men to their duties was proverbial; Kentuckians would say of a day of especially foul weather that no one would be abroad "but crows and Methodist ministers."[77]

Grant Galloway and his Progeny

Samuel Galloway gave $1,000, a considerable sum in those days, to each of his sons as they reached 21 years of age. Grant married Alice Moreland the year he reached that milestone, and used the money to buy a farm just north of Falmouth, Kentucky. He bought the farm from his brother George, who moved to Bourbon County, which had shrunken considerably from its original expanse, as other counties were carved out of it. In 1897, Grant followed him there. He rented a farm for a few years, then bought George's farm when the restless George moved out to Oklahoma territory. Over the years, Grant would buy and sell several farms, but he stayed in Bourbon County.

Looking back in his last years, (he lived to be 84), he said that he would have liked to have been a lawyer. But he had little chance for education and farming was to be his lot. The battles he fought were with economic recessions, droughts, insects, and erratic crop prices, enemies that his hard work, frugality and intelligence could not overcome.

Grant lived a quiet life, but didn't lack the Galloway spirit, as one incident proves. His sister Mary had married a ne'er-do-well who mistreated her and the children until, dying of tuberculosis, she moved back with her family. When the sixteen-year-old Grant saw her spouse approaching the house, he took a shot at him. The boy was indicted, tried, convicted- - and fined one cent. [78]

Grant saw hard times, but he kept his land and his pride. He and his wife Alice farmed and prayed and raised eight children according to their strict standards of decency, believing that to spare the rod was to spoil the child. The children grew up in comparative poverty, as did most offspring of small farmers; this writer's father remembered years when his only Christmas present was a pair of socks knitted by his Mother.

Of their eight children, the eldest (Gertrude) died in infancy. The next was a daughter, Mildred, who never married, but became a milliner who owned a shop in Rome, Georgia. Their first son, Floyd Emerson, was a career military officer. The next, Roy Clark, owned a farm in Paris, was President of the County Farm Bureau, an elder in his church, a cornerstone of civic groups, and president of a citizens' committee that sent Paris' leading politician to prison for stuffing ballot boxes. Finnell became a prominent banker in Maysville, whose hobby was raising prizewinning dahlias. Mabel made a respectable marriage but died soon after her first child was born. Jesse became a railroad engineer, (a sought-after occupation in those days when rails were sinews that tied the country together) and Miriam married one. The youngest, Everett, never settled to a career.

All of the children except the two eldest daughters married and produced children. Miriam had two daughters and Mabel had one son. Roy's son held an administrative job with the telephone company and his two daughters were secretaries. Finnell's two sons were engineers, although one- the Thomas to whom we are indebted for so much genealogical data- later became a stockbroker and a realtor. Jesse produced a large brood, some of whom sported carrot-colored hair. One of his sons became a doctor in Paris and tended his Uncle Roy and Aunt Martha during their final illnesses. Another had problems adjusting to peace after meritorious service in World War II, so ran afoul of the law and landed in prison, where he pioneered in *pro se* prisoner litigation; (he was born into the wrong generation, for he undoubtedly would have flourished in James Galloway's time and place).

The family lived near Paris on a farm with a small, white frame house surrounded by a white picket fence and flower beds. This writer remembers a litter of kittens up in the loft of a barn that held, according to the season, the sweet smell of hay or the acrid aroma of tobacco; the subterranean dimness of an icehouse, where jars of canned vegetables and preserves glittered on dim shelves; the soft fuzz of new-hatched ducklings, brought in to keep warm beside the cast-iron stove; hunting for nests where anxious hens had hidden their eggs; sacks of flour, printed in dainty floral patterns that would later be turned into clothes or quilts when the flour was used up; a Sycamore-bordered stream, where the cows came to drink; the smothering softness of a feather bed; country memories, as timeless as they used to be common.

The small house was always spotlessly clean. One room was kept as a parlor, used only on such special occasions as when it was the family's turn to host the preacher at Sunday dinner and, since it was not usually heated, to dry apple slices for pie. In the middle of the room was a table which held the family Bible. A picture of the oldest child, who died as a baby, hung on the wall, painted from a tintype by an itinerant artist. The bedrooms were furnished with feather beds, made by Alice from her own chickens and covered with carefully-quilted comforters. Nothing was ever wasted: not time nor words nor worldly goods. There wasn't enough of anything to spare.

Floyd Emerson Galloway

This history will close with some notes on Grant's oldest son and this writer's father, Floyd Emerson Galloway. Born September 11, 1890, he carried on the pioneering spirit that distinguished his ancestors.

Like his father and grandfather before him, he grew up on a Kentucky farm. But he was not content with this kind of life, so put himself through the University of Kentucky by taking a tobacco crop each summer and working in the library during the school term. Neither of his parents had gone to college, and only two of his siblings would even enter one, but he knew that that college offered the best way to get ahead.

Emerson (he never used the name Floyd; in fact, we don't know why his parents dropped the fine old family names and came up with the odd assortment they gave to their children) was slighty-built, but scrappy. His larger, if younger, brother Roy would recall how he would often have to intervene to settle scraps that "Em" had started. In college, he was on the football team until broken bones took him out, but his athletic prowess was based on speed and spunkiness, not size. He was six feet tall and broad-shouldered, but small-boned and skinny: the typical Galloway build. He also had the typical Galloway coloring of light blue eyes and fine, sandy hair.

In 1914, when he was about to graduate from college, he saw a civil service ad for experts to grade hemp in the Philippines. All he knew about those Islands was that they were far away from the farm, and that was where he wanted to be. He knew enough about hemp to convince the government that he was the man they needed, for this was a major local crop, used to make rope and protected for many years by a tariff that Henry Clay had gotten through Congress. So young Galloway said goodbye to college, farm, and family and set off on the long trip to the Islands. At the time he left, it is doubtful if he had been outside of Kentucky; when he returned six years later, he would have been around the world.

The next three years were spent in the Philippines, riding his motorcycle along jungle trails, twice breaking his nose in falls; sailing to remote islands, often in native boats; living for weeks off of native food and canned salmon; developing a contempt for self-serving missionaries, but respect for Singer sewing machine salesmen, who penetrated as deep as he did into the jungles; meeting Tagalog head-hunters (he took a snapshot of natives displaying a captive hung from a pole- *sans* head); and he undoubtedly did a good job of grading hemp.

The farm boy's travels covered much of the spread-out Islands, which, coincidentally, his future father-in-law, Colonel Cornelius Gardenier, had helped bring under American control after the Spanish-American War. Once he was on an island where the only link to the outside world was a boat that came once a month. He woke up on that day to hear his native servant chanting softly, "senor, wake up," and to see the boat pulling out of the harbor. The native had been afraid to wake him quickly, fearing that the soul, which he thought left the body during sleep, would not have time to get back in place.

In April of 1917, America declared war on Germany. Galloway, then 27 years old, went to a recruiting station in Manila and signed up, no doubt expecting to sail for Europe and the battlefields of France. But the army moves in mysterious ways; instead of heading for France, he was given a Captain's commission and shipped off to Siberia, in command of an infantry company. Instead of fighting Germans, the men found themselves fighting Russians, with whom America was not even at war. To make matters even stranger, his company was composed of Italian soldiers.

This peculiar incident in our history merits a brief digression. Galloway was part of what one author has called "the unknown war with Russia."[79] The tzarist regime had been overthrown and the prevailing Bolshevik party had signed a peace treaty with Germany, so as to concentrate on trying to put down its internal enemies, collectively known as the "Whites." The allies pressured President Wilson to intervene, for various reasons: to protect the enormous amount of supplies, sent by America while Russia was still in the war, that had accumulated in Vladivostok; to rescue the 50,000 or so Czechoslovakian troops who were trapped in Russia by the German lines; to protect the Trans-Siberian railroad, which was the only way out for them; and to keep the Japanese from going in on their own, in which case they might decide not to leave.

President Wilson resisted, fearing that the Russian people might view intervention as an invasion. Although he was personally anti-Bolshevik, America did not officially take sides in the Revolution. But, in July of 1918, Wilson, in an ambiguously-worded memo, directed that American troops be sent to Siberia to "steady any efforts at self-government in which Russia was willing to accept assistance." With General William Graves in command, the 27th and 31st Infantry Regiments, which had been stationed in the Philippines, arrived in Siberia with about 5,000 men and 100 officers. Captain Galloway's 2nd Italian U.S. Army troops probably joined him there; altogether, the Allies sent almost 100,000 men to Siberia: Italians, French, Japanese, French, and British as well as American.

On their arrival in Vladivostok, the U.S. Siberian Expeditionary Force encountered chaos. There were military and civil personnel from a dozen nations in the city, often working at cross-purposes, with no one in charge. The government had broken down. None of the competing factions could command much popular support. Piles of Allied military goods lay around, unsecured. The situation did not improve with time.

An Armistice was signed in November of 1919, ending the war with Germany, but not changing the situation in Siberia. The corrupt and ineffective White government, under Admiral Kolchak, had fallen and its army had disintegrated. The Allies debated whether to recognize the Bolshevik regime or to invade and try to topple it. In the end, they did neither. In the spring of 1920, the American troops were withdrawn.

The Americans' primary role had been to guard the rail lines and the coal fields that fueled the trains. The troops were frequently under attack by Cossacks and pro-Bolshevik guerillas, and often in sub-zero temperatures. (A snapshot of Captain Galloway and some other officers shows them bundled up in fur coats, with earmuffs and enormous mittens). Not only were 353 men of this Expeditionary Force killed, but it served under combat conditions longer than any other American force involved in World War I.

The war over, Galloway and his company left Siberia on a troopship, sailing home by way of the Suez Canal and the Mediterranean, where his Italian troops were disembarked. By the time he was back in America, the farm boy had been around the world. He brought a few souvenirs: a dog named Alto, who had been his companion in Siberia but was stolen on the way home; a stuffed and mounted head of a rare sheep he'd shot that, in years to come, graced his home until moths took their toll; a finely engraved Russian silver spoon; and some exquisite cloisonné enamel bowls, acquired when his troopship stopped in China. He also brought back a taste for military life.

He inherited his ancestors' pioneering spirit and, like them, he chose the challenge of the frontier, which was now in the sky. He entered the Air Service Pilots School, where he was called "Pops" because he was considerably older than his classmates, in 1921, then went on to the Observation School. On graduating in 1922, he was assigned to Washington, D.C. as pilot to the Assistant Secretary of War. In 1929, he married Martha Gardener, the daughter of a regular Army Infantry Colonel, Cornelius Gardenier, son of a Dutch Reformed Church minister who had brought his congregation to Holland, Michigan, while Cornelius was an infant. Martha's widowed mother, Bessie Patton Gardenier, had brought her two daughters to Washington, where Martha got a Master's degree from George Washington University while enjoying the city's social whirl.

Aviation was a glamorous and dangerous occupation. When Galloway would fly home to visit his family's Kentucky farm, landing his flimsy biplane in a ploughed field, crowds of townspeople would drive out to see the miraculous machine. He and his fellow pilots delighted in dangerous stunts like doing loop-the-loops and flying under telegraph wires. He flew airmail over the Rockies, a death-defying job in those pre-radar days, when the pilot had to rely on his own skills to keep from crashing into a mountainside veiled by clouds.

His distinguished military career spanned thirty years, as the Army Air Service evolved into the Army Air Corps and then the Air Force. The military sent him to their best schools: the Air Corps Tactical School, the Army War College, and the Command and General Staff School. He was given command of airfields: Crissy (San Francisco), Boeing (Tacoma, Washington), Maxwell (Montgomery, Alabama), Bolling (Washington, D.C.), and Albrook (Panama). Promoted to Brigadier General during World War II, he organized and commanded the Air Force Service Command in the Caribbean area.

On retirement, he bought a farm in Paris, Kentucky, a place his ancestors had helped to found, and that holds so much Galloway history. He died there died in 1955, survived by three children: a son, named after him, who had a daughter named Martha and a son with the same name; Mary Ann, who had daughters named Mary Whiting, Patton, and Anne Shelby; and Patton, who had a daughter named Barendina and a son named Charles Samuel, and who is the author of this family history.

A Final Note

To cast this story as a Cautionary Tale, I will close with an observation from Alexis de Tocqueville's classic commentary on *Democracy in America*, written in the 1830's:

Among aristocratic nations, as families remain for centuries in the same condition, often on the same spot, all generations become, as it were, contemporaneous. A man almost always knows his forefathers and respects them; he thinks he already sees his remote descendants and he loves them. He willingly imposes duties on himself toward the former and the latter, and he will frequently sacrifice his personal gratifications to those who went before and to those who will come after him. .

Among democratic nations new families are constantly springing up, others are constantly falling away, and all that remain change their condition; the woof of time is every instant broken and the track of generations effaced. Those who went before are soon forgotten; of those who will come after, no one has any idea: the interest of man is confined to those in close propinquity to himself. . . . They owe nothing to any man, they expect nothing from any man; they acquire the habit of always considering themselves as standing alone, and they are apt to imagine that their whole destiny is in their own hands.

Thus not only does democracy make every man forget his ancestors, but it hides his descendants and separates his contemporaries from him; it throws him back forever upon himself alone and threatens in the end to confine him entirely within the solitude of his own heart.

Footnotes

The following abbreviations are used:

GPC for Baltimore: Genealogical Publishing Company.

PMHB for *Pennsylvania Magazine of History and Biography.*

PP for privately published.

HB for Westminster, Maryland: Heritage Books, which includes Willow Bend Books.

1. George F. Black, *The Surnames of Scotland.* (New York: New York Public Library, 1962), quoting from William Stewart's version of the *History of Scotland* by Hector Boece.

2. *Ibid.* Other London spellings were Golywe and Goliwey.

3. The settlement of Ulster by Scots involved various phases, over many years, and is beyond the scope of this paper. Sources used include Wayland F. Dunway, *The Scotch Irish of Colonial America* (Chapel Hill: University of North Carolina Press, 1944); *Encyc. Britannica,* which calls James' Plantation "the most successful British settlement made in Ireland" and says that "The newcomers were mainly from the Scottish Lowlands;" and Charles A. Hannah, *The Scotch Irish* (GPC, 1985).

4. James A. Froude, a noted English historian, wrote that "religious bigotry, commercial jealousy, and modern landlordism had combined to do their worst against the Ulster settlement. . .In the two years which followed the Antrim evictions [in 1772], thirty thousand Protestants left Ulster for a land where there was no legal robbery, and where those who sowed the seed could reap the harvest. They went with bitterness in their hearts." *The English in Ireland in the Eighteenth Century,* II (NY: 1878), p. 125.

5. Ruth H. Deverter, *Our Pioneer Ancestors: The Scotts and the Galloways* (Daytown, Texas: PP, 1959), p. 198, giving as her sole source a Charles Mills Galloway, Jr. of Washington, D.C..

6. David Hackett Fischer, *Albion's Seed: Four British Folkways* (NY: Oxford University Press 1969).

7. Since Maryland and Virginia were settled by Englishmen who brought with them the English legal system and who were obligated to report back to their sponsors in England, careful parish and county records were kept. This was not true in later settlements like Kentucky.

8. N. M. Nugent, *Cavaliers and Pioneers* (Richmond: Virginia State Library, 1975) V. 3, p. 83.

9. Peter W. Coldham, *English Adventurers and Emigrants 1609-1660.* (GPC, 1984).

10. Oliver LaFarge, *A Pictorial History of the American Indian*, (NY: Crown Publishers, 1956), p. 31.

11. Carl Bridenbaugh, *Jamestown 1544-1699* (NY: Oxford University Press, 1980), p. 45.

12. G.M. Trevelyan, *Illustrated English Social History*, v. II (London: Longmans, Green and Co., 1942), p. 69.

13. H.D. Richardson, *Side-Lights on Maryland History,* (Baltimore: Williams and Wilkins, 1967), p.37. Amateur histories often include transcripts of original documents that would otherwise be left in obscurity, as well as recorded recollections that contain at least a germ of fact and give flavor to better-documented facts.

14. Beverly Fleet, *Virginia Colonial Abstracts.* (GPC, 1988).

15. Information on Nansemond is primarily from Evelyn Cross, *Nansemond Chronicles 1606-1800, Abstracts Taken From Quaker Records in Nansemond County Courthouse* (typescript in N.C. Archives and History Department Genealogy Library, undated).

16. Peter W. Coldham, *The Bristol Register of Servants Sent to Foreign Plantations 1654-865.* (GPC, 1988); Ellen French, *List of Emigrants to America from Liverpool 1697-1702* (GPC, 1969). "The need for a scrupulous tally of indentured servants arose from the long-standing and notorious practice of kidnapping, inveigling and bribing youngsters onto ships bound for the labour-hungry colonies, there to be sold at a good profit."

17. Robert Barnes, *Baltimore County Families 1659-1759*, (GPC, 1989) says that William Galloway was in Baltimore County by 1705, when he was named in the will of his son William, and may be the man who witnessed a will in December of 1675.

18. Beverly Fleet, *supra* Note 14; William Hopkins, *Virginia Wills and Administration* (Richmond: PP, 1987).

19. Peter W. Coldham, *Emigrants from England to the American Colonies 1773-1776 (GPC,* 1988*)* and *Bonded Passengers to America, V. III.* (GPC, 1983).

20. Wesley Frank Craven, *The Southern Colonies in the Seventeenth Century 1607-1689* (Louisiana State University Press, 1970), p. 234; Joseph B. Dunn, *History of Nansemond County* (PP, n.d.).

21. Joshua D. Warfield *Founders of Anne Arundel and Howard Counties* (Baltimore: Kohn and Pollick 1905), 109-10.

22. Some of the sources for data on the Galloways in Maryland are listed here. These include both compilations of official records and family histories. Most facts stated in the text are supported by several of these and other sources, and it is not practicable to cite a source for each statement.

    Jane Baldwin, *Maryland Calendar of Wills,* 8 vol.(HP, 1991);

    Gaius Brumbaugh, *Maryland Records- Colonial, Revolutionary, County and Church, from original sources* (Baltimore: Wilkins, 1915);

    Robert Barnes, *Baltimore County Deed Abstracts, 1659-1750*(HP, 1996); *1783 Tax List of Baltimore County* (HP, 1995); *Baltimore County Families, 1659-1759* (GPC, 1989); *Maryland Marriages 1634-1777,*(GPC, 1975);

    B.S. Carothers. *Index of Baltimore County Wills,* (PP, 1964);

R.B. Clark, *Baltimore County Tax List 1699-1706* (PP, 1964); *Index to Cecil County Wills* (PP, 1981).

Peter Coldham, *Settlers of Maryland 1679-1700,* GPC, 1995); Jane Cotton, *The Maryland Calendar of Wills , 16 volumes,*(FLP, 1988):

Rosemary Dodd and Patricia Bausell, *Abstracts of Land Records in Anne Arundel County Maryland,* (Pasadena, Md.: AA County Genelogical Society, n.d.), 7 vol..

Robert Hall, *Land Grants in the Middle Neck Hundred of Anne Arundel County 1650-1704* (HB, 2001).

J. R. Jacobsen, *Quaker Records In Maryland* (Annapolis: Hall of Records, 1966).

Leslie and Neil Keddie, *Baltimore County Wills* (HB, 2002).

Calvin and Mary Mowbray*, Early Settlers of Dorchester County and their Lands* (PP, 1982*).*

Rev. E.D. Neill, *The Founders of Maryland* (Albany: Joel Munsell, 1876).

Harry Newman, *Anne Arundel Gentry,* (Annapolis: PP, 1970).

Henry Peden, *Inhabitants of Baltimore County 1692-1763, 1763-1774,* (HP,1989).

Thomas Scharf, *History of Baltimore City and County* (Philadelphia: L. H. Everts, 1881).

Gus Skordas, *The Early Settlers of Maryland: index to Names of Immigrants Compiled from Records of land Patents 1633-80.* GPC, 1960) .

Joshua Warfield, Founders of Anne Arundel and Howard Counties (Baltimore: Kohn and Pollick 1905).

23. J.R. Jacobsen, *Quaker Records in Maryland, supra* note 22. Quote is from Neill, *supra* note 22, p. 144.

24. Richardson, *supra* note 13, p. 223. Neill, *supra* Note 22, quoting contemporary sources, says that Eliza Harris, wife of a prosperous London merchant, was preaching in Maryland as early as 1657. In the autumn of 1663, two Quaker women were preaching in Calvert County; they were back from New England where they "suffered thirty two stripes apiece, with a nine corded whip, three knots in each cord, being drawn up to the pillory in such an uncivil manner, as is not to be rehearsed, with a running knot about their hands, the very first lash of which, drew the blood, and made it run down in abundance from their breasts."

25. "Richard Galloway, the son of Samuell [sic.] and Ann Galloway, was born in London in the Kingdom of England the llth month and 5th day of 1689." (West River Quaker Records, quoted in H.W. Newman, *To Maryland from Overseas; (*Annapolis: PP, n.d.).

26. Peter Brock, *Pioneers of the Peaceable Kingdom,* (Princeton University Press, 1968), p.38.

27. Peter Coldham, *King's Passengers to Maryland and Virginia* (HP, 1997).

28. George Johnston, *History of Cecil County*, Maryland. (PP, 1881).

29. Charles Keith, *Provincial Councillors of Pennsylvania,* (Philadelphia: Sharp Printing Co., 1883) 325-331.

30. Richard Pratt, *a Treasury of Early American Homes* (NY: McGraw Hill, 1946), p.55.

31. Reaney Kelly, "Tulip Hill, Its History and Its People, 60 *Maryland Historical Magazine*, Dec., 1965, pp. 357-9; Karen Green, *The Maryland Gazette: Genealogical and Historical Abstracts* (Galveston: Frontier Press, 1989).

32. Penn*sylvania Archives*, Minutes of Provincial Council for June 15, 1769.

33. William Eddis, *Letters from America*, (Cambridge: Belknap Press, 1969).

34. Estate of John Gassaway, cited in Harry W. Newman, *Supra* Note 22.

35. "The Ancestry and Earlier Life of George Washington," *Pennsylvania Magazine of History and Biography*, v. 16, p. 297.

36. Henry Peden, *Quaker Records of Baltimore and Harford Counties 1801-1825* (HP, 2000).

37. Dunway, *supra* note 3.

38. Information on this settlement is from Uriah James Jones, *History of the Early Settlement of the Juniata Valley.* (1889, reprinted 1940 by Telegraph Press, Harrisburg), and *History of that Part of the Susquehannah and Juniata valleys, embraced in the counties of Mifflin, Juniata, Perry, Union and Snyder, in the Commonwealth of Pennsylvania*, edited by F. Ellis and A. N. Hungerford, (Philadelphia: Everts, Peck & Richards, 1886, pp. 846-865).

39. *Pennsylvania Archives, Volume I,* p. 643. The Proclamation and Peters' report are given in full in the *Archives*, which also show that Peters was in the area on that date.

40. Thomas Balch (ed.), *Letters and Papers Relating Chiefly to the*

Provincial History of Pennsylvania, (Philadelphia: Cressy & Marking, 1855), 189.

41. Deverter, *Supra* Note 5; Roy Stevenson King, *The Ancestral Pilgrimage Along Life's Pathway* (1939: no publisher given); reprinted in the Paris, Kentucky, *Kentuckian Citizen* for Feb. 19, 1946; Rev. Robert Simpson, *History of the Covenators* (no publisher or date given). (Incidentally, King cites as a major source a "History of the Susquehanna and Juniata Valley," without giving a date or publisher; he presumably means the history cited *supra* note 38, which he not only mistitles, but misquotes, again showing his lack of reliability.

42. Brian Mitchell, ed., *Irish Immigration Lists* 1833-1839, (HP, 1988) lists two Galloways who give their religion as Covenanters, Robert (b. 1816) and James (b. 1814), both of whom left Anoghill Parish in Southwest Antrim County for St. Johns in 1836, much too late to fit into our family tree.

43. James Logan, quoted in Hannah, *Supra* note 3, p. 63.

44. The quote from the Gazette is given in J. Daniel Rupp, *History of Lancaster and York Counties* (Lancaster: Gilbert Hills, 1845), 586. King, *supra* note 41, quoted the *Gazette* as saying that those killed included "Elizabeth Galloway, mother of George and William, also William's wife and two children," and that one Galloway son escaped after he saw his grandmother shot down and other settlers taken prisoner. However, the article actually gives the names of the murdered as Elizabeth Gallway [*sic*.], Henry Gibson, Robert Peer, William Berryhill, and David M'Clelland. Missing were John Martin's wife and two children, and a young woman; Charles Stewart's wife and two children; David M'Clelland's wife and two children. William Fleming and wife were taked prisoners; Fleming's son, and one Hicks, were killed and scalped.

45. Sidney G. Fisher, *the Quaker Colonies* (New Haven: Yale University Press, 1919) p. 9 James Logan, quoted in Hannah, *Supra*

note 3, p. 63.

46. This is from a narrative of James Galloway, Sr., taken at his residence in Greene County, Ohio, in October 1832 by his grandson Albert Galloway, and was included in King, supra Note 41; also filed at the DAR shrine, Duncan Tavern, in Paris, Kentucky. Where King includes actual manuscripts, such as the Galloway memoir, these are presumed to be accurate; his undocumented statements, such as the origins of the Pennsylvania Galloways, are not. Some events in James' life, such as his military service and land purchases, are documented by official sources.

47. David Dobson, *Directory of Scottish Settlers in North America 1625-1825,* (GPC, 1985); source listed as Public Records Office, London.

48. Viola Root Cameron, *Emigrants from Scotland to America 1774-75, copied from a loose bundle of treasury papers in the Public Records Office, London* (Baltimore: Southern Book Company, 1959).

49. The Pennsylvania Galloways are: George (1723-1786), m. Rebecca Junkin; James (1750-1838), m. Rebecca Junkin; (this is not a typo; George's son James married a Rebecca Junkin, presumably his cousin, and two of his sisters married Junkins); James (1758-1840), m. Jane Bailey; John (1750-1780), m. Mary Harrison; John (1746-1782), m. Mary Cummings; Joseph (1750-1790) m. Mary Galloway; Joseph (1757-1838) m. (1) Isabelle Orr (2) Polly Cross; Robert (?-1790); Samuel (1747-1814) ; William (1743-1795) m. (1) Catherine Thompson (2) Rebecca Mitchell). The birthdates show that, in 1776, these men ranged in age from 18 to 53, so that several generations were included. Also, three of the men were born in the same year, so were probably not brothers. All except John, who was a Lieutenant, served as privates in the Army.

Four of the 19 "patriots" are familiar names from Maryland: Joseph (1750-1790), m. Mary Galloway (he served with the rank of Major;

Marshall (1760-1827) m. Hannah Watlin; Moses (1726-1798) m. (1) Mary Nicholson (2) Pamelia Owings; William, Jr. (1738-1801) m. Ann Waller.

50. Most writings about Galloway are concerned with his politics; the best biographical source is Ernest Baldwin, "Joseph Galloway, the Loyalist Politician," *PMHB* 26 (1902) 161-91; 289-94; 417-42.

51. Joseph Galloway, *Letters to a Nobleman on the Conduct of the War in the Middle Colonies.* (London: J. Wilkie, 1830), 59-60.

52. Edward H. Tatum (ed.) *The American Journal of Ambrose Searle,* (San Marion: Huntington Library, 1940).

53. Grace Growden's wartime diary, edited by Raymond Werner, was published in the *PMHB*, v. 55 (1931) and 58 (1958). Their only child, Betsay, was able to recoup part of her fortune through legal action after the war. She married an Englishman and settled permanently in that country.

54. Harold B. Hancock, *The Loyalists of Revolutionary Delaware,* (Newark: University of Delaware Press, 1977).

55. Henry Peden, *Revolutionary Patriots of Baltimore and Baltimore County* (FLP, 1988), p. 95-6; Kelly, *supra* note 31 at 375.

56. See James' Journal, *supra* Note 46.

57. Told by Squire George Galloway of Xenia, Ohio, who was a child at the fort, and quoted in King, *supra* note 41; see also James Galloway, Note 46, and an article from the August 1988 *Xenia Daily Gazette* on file in the DAR library in Paris, Kentucky.

58. Journal of Lt. Colonel A. Hugley, Commander 11th Pennsylvania Reg't, July, 1779; *PMHB*, v.33 (1909), p. 410.

59. W.R. Jillson, *Kentucky Land Grants,* (Louisville: 1925)

60. Maryland patents, certs., and warrants- #133-17777-84, Hall of Records, Annapolis, Maryland., p. 745.

61. A family bible of a Maryland Thomas Galloway shows births from 1806-1817 of children named Moses, Mary Elizabeth, Thomas; since our Thomas' grandson Thomas was born in 1787, these are probably his children. *Maryland Genelogical Society Bulletin,* v. 28 (1986).

62. Elihu's dates are well documented. U.S. Census records for Jennings County, Indiana show an "Elihue" Galloway who was born in Maryland and who was age 66 in 1850 and 76 in 1860. We have copies of the application and grant of 120 acres for Bounty Land under the Act of 3rd March, 1855, for his service in the War of 1812, which includes a certification from the Bourbon County, Kentucky, Clerk as to his marriage on March 2, 1812.

63. Anne Fitzgerald, ed., *Kentucky Ancestors,* v. 19, No 2, (October 1983).

64. James Ford's Journal, v. 63, *PMHB*, Jan.1940, 14.

65. Data from Maryland Hall of Records.

66. Office of Bourbon County Circuit Clerk, Chancery suits filed May 17, 1803 and December, 1804.

67. V.D. White, *Index to War of 1812 Pension Files* (Waynesboro, Tennessee: National Historical Publications), p. 785. Daniel (m. Sarah) was a private in Captain McAffee's Kentucky Militia; John (m. 1st, Mary, 2nd, Augusta) lived in Baltimore, served in Wilson's Virginia Militia and d. 1848; John (m. Jane Humphry in Mifflin County. Pennsylvania) served in Pennsylvania. Militia and d. 1855 in Ashland City, Ohio; Samuel (m. Elizabeth Collins) lived in

Greene County. Ohio and served in Ohio Rangers. Elihu is listed as "Elihu or Elihue."

68. G. Glenn Clift, *Remember the Raisin!* (Frankfort: Kentucky Historical Society, 1961).

69. E. G. Barton Collection of Northern Kentucky Families papers], in Falmouth, Ky., public library, citing interview with Joseph Galloway (youngest son of Samuel Galloway), 1937. (copies provided by Thomas Roddy Galloway).

70. Maurice Holmes, *Early Landowners of Jennings County, Indiana.* (Shelbyville, Indiana: 1876).

71. Henry and Elizabeth Wyatt were married in Spottsylvania County, Virginia; the date is variously recorded as from 1780 to 1787.

72. E. G. Barton Collection, *supra* Note 69.

73. Bell Irvin Wiley, *The Life of Billy Yank*, (Baton Rouge: Louisiana State University, 1952) p. 198, quotes from his diary.

74. Information on this French connection was furnished by Thomas Roddy Galloway, including: William G. Sibley, *The French Five Hundred and Other Papers,* (Gallipolis, the Tribune Press, 1901); James P. Averill, *History of Gallia County.* (from photocopied pages which do not give publisher or date).

75. *The Speeches, Addresses and Writings of Cassius M. Clay, Jr.* (NY: the Winthrop Press, 1914).

76. A 1766 will (executed in 1773) of Philip Morland, Charles County, left 143 acres to his sons Phillip and Stephen and wife Lelia; "Richard Morland, heir at law, refused to attend probate of will." *Magruder's Maryland Colonial Abstracts*, (GPC, 1968). (Note the varied spelling of the name, as is common). See Also "the Moreland

Family Bible with Grimsley Records," *St. Louis Genelogical Quarterly*, (March, 1968).

77. James G. Leyburn, *The Scotch Irish*, (Chapel Hill: University of North Carolina, 1962), 284.

78. This incident, and numerous other references, were collected by Thomas Roddy Galloway from family and other sources.

79. Robert Maddox, *The Unknown War With Russia*, (San Rafael: Presidio Press, 1977); Christine Putnam, "AEF Siberia," Doughboy Center; see website, by the Great War Society.